God Still Heals

Keys to Activate God's Healing Power in Your Life

Dr. Andrea I. Hart

God Still Heals. By Dr. Andrea I. Hart
Published by Agapelife Health & Healing Solutions
3545 St. Johns Bluff Ed. S. #1-214
Jacksonville, Florida 32224
www.drandreaihart.com

Email: contact@drandreaihart.com
Website: www.drandreaihart.com
Facebook: God Still Heals with Dr. Andrea
Instagram: dr_andreaihart
Twitter/Periscope: dr_andreaihart

Unless otherwise noted, all Scripture quotations are from the King James Version of the Bible and marked KJV.

Scriptures marked AMP are taken from the AMPLIFIED BIBLE (AMP): Scripture taken from the AMPLIFIED® BIBLE, Copyright © 1954, 1958, 1962, 1964, 1965, 1987 by the Lockman Foundation Used by Permission. (www.Lockman.org)

Scriptures marked CEV are taken from the CONTEMPORARY ENGLISH VERSION (CEV): Scripture taken from the CONTEMPORARY ENGLISH VERSION copyright© 1995 by the American Bible Society. Used by permission.

Scriptures marked GNB are taken from the GOOD NEWS BIBLE (GNB): Scriptures taken from the Good News Bible © 1994 published by the Bible Societies/HarperCollins Publishers Ltd UK, Good News Bible© American Bible Society 1966, 1971, 1976, 1992. Used with permission.

Scriptures marked ISV are taken from the INTERNATIONAL

Cover design by PixelStudio
Visit the authors website at www.drandreaihart.com

Receive free book bonuses at:
http://bit.ly/gshbookbonus (password: healing)

Individuals and church groups may order books from Dr. Andrea I. Hart directly via contact@drandreaihart.com. Retailers and wholesalers should order from our distributors.

Printed in the United States of America
ISBN: 978-0-578-46241-7

DEDICATION

I DEDICATE THIS BOOK to anyone who has believed God for healing and it seems as if He has not heard you. My prayer is that this book will provide the needed answers and freedom to live a full life, healed and whole.

Contents

Acknowledgements

I would like to thank all of those who supported me through the process of completing this book. My husband, Royce Hart, Jr., family – parents Alvin & Ernestine, sister Dr. Lauren Carroll, parents-in-love, Steve & Mary Holmes, my best sister-friend, Kimberly Austin, my church family at Impact Church – Jacksonville, Florida (especially the Prayer & Healing Team), and my pastors, Bishop George and April Davis. I also would like to thank the numerous people along the way who encouraged me in my writing gifts and calling. Thank you!

INTRODUCTION

DOES GOD STILL HEAL in this day and time? Why do so many people die with sickness and disease? Is God trying to teach me something though this ordeal with sickness? Is God punishing me with this? These are all relevant questions that we often ask God when faced with sickness and disease. These are questions that I have asked myself when presented with sickness in those close to me. In this book you will find the answers to these questions and others which might come up when presented with pain, sickness, or disease in your body. In this book we examine healing as a holistic journey encompassing spirit, soul, and body. This book provides tools, strategies and guidance for spiritual and physical health, healing, and well-being. We identify emotional, mental, generational, and demonic roots and strongholds which could be contributing to the sickness or disease you currently might face.

I wrote this book as a foundation for those who have been seeking God for healing. I have been working with individuals profession-ally and in the ministry in the area of health and healing since 1999. In my own life, my husband Royce and I sought the Lord for years concerning healing for End-Stage Renal Disease and Type 1 Diabetes. You can find our testimony on my website www. drandreaihart.com/testimony. I have worked with individuals in schools of healing interceding and teaching others to appropriate faith for healing. Professionally, I have advanced degrees in heath and education and have spent time teaching patients and health professionals to live healthy lifestyles. I am nationally certified to teach health education and have held teaching and research appointments at state universities for many years. However, these are not my greatest qualifications. My greatest qualification is a heart to see the healing power of God manifest in every individual in need of healing and that they live in divine health.

I personally believe it is the combination of "God's super on your natural" that causes lasting change to occur in your life. I wrote this book so that those suffering will know that they do not have to submit and live with sickness and disease. God is still healing today! This book is your start to building a solid foundation of faith in this area.

I have been able to put these keys into practice in my own life and in many others lives whom I have been able to teach these principles. This book includes what I have learned over the past 15 years of study and training in this area.

Book Features

As an educator by trade for the last 18 years, I would be remiss to not include a few teaching tools in this book! Within these pages you will find the following:

- *Book Bonus Material.* Access to dynamic supporting materials on this book's bonus website. This includes video teachings, guides/eBooks, devotionals, and more. You can go to http://bit.ly/gshbookbonus to access these resources (even without reading this book...my gift to you).

- *Activation Prayers.* Included at the end of each chapter. These prayers are designed for you to read and believe to activate the power of God concerning the keys discussed in the chapter.

- *Next Steps.* Actions steps are always needed to apply what we have just read. These steps are short actionable items that you can complete which will help you gain a greater understanding of the keys presented in the chapter.

- *Prescriptions for Divine Health.* These are natural keys to living a healthy life. Divine health includes using natural wisdom to help lead and guide us to making smart decisions concerning stewardship of our greatest possession, our bodies. These keys will help you to not live in fear of the unknown concerning your health but be able to soundly take care of your body. More prescriptions for divine health can be found on my website www.drandreaihart.com.

Thank you for the opportunity to speak into your life though this book. My prayer is that you will take the information found in these pages and grow in wisdom, knowledge, and understanding about yourself. I pray you will also share this understanding with someone else so that they too can live in divine health.

-- Andrea I. Hart, EdD, MPH, CHES

Chapter 1

Is Healing God's Will?

Is healing God's will? In Christianity, this has been a hotly contested subject depending on your faith background. There are certain faiths that believe that the supernatural went away with the apostles. They believe that healing, signs, wonders, and miracles are no longer happening today. If you know and understand the character of God, you could not possibly believe this to be the truth. Why would a loving God leave His people to suffer due to sin, sickness, and disease? Why would God leave us on this earth to be tormented by the devil in these areas? God provided a solution. He provided an escape route regarding the issues of this life. Not believing that God wants you to live an abundant life in health and prosperity is a lie from the enemy. The Bible also discusses this in 3 John 2.

> *Beloved, I pray that you may prosper in all things and be in health, just as your soul prospers.*
>
> -- 3 John 2

The word prosper in the original Greek gives the connotation of a successful journey[1]. Our lives can be seen as a journey. It is God's expectation for us to be successful and live in divine health. The word "health" in that scripture means complete wholeness with nothing lacking[2]. It impacts your well-being *and* your prosperity. God wants you well. It is easier to fulfill the purpose God has for your life with a well body, mind, will, and emotions than to be sick battling disease. We serve a good God, which gives good gifts to His children (Matthew 7:11). Healing and prosperity are both good gifts.

First things first, to walk and minister the healing power of God in your life, you must settle the fact in your heart that *it's God will to heal!* It is not only God's will to heal, but it is God's will to heal YOU!

> *Surely He has borne our griefs and carried our sorrows; yet we esteemed Him stricken, smitten by God, and afflicted. But He was wounded for our transgressions, He was bruised for our iniquities; The chastisement for our peace was upon Him, And by His stripes we are healed.*
>
> -- Isaiah 53:4-5

> *Who Himself bore our sins in His own body on the tree, that we, having died to sins, might live for righteousness—by whose stripes you were healed.*
>
> -- 1 Peter 2:24

Our healing was purchased on the cross of Christ over 2000 years ago. We just have to receive by faith that which was already done for us. The most obvious question that should come to mind is how do I do that? How do I receive my healing by faith?

Well, I am glad you asked that! To answer that question, we have to address what is your definition of faith? It takes Bible faith to receive the promises of God. Faith is simply what you believe. Bible faith is what you believe based upon the Word of God. In society today, there are many counterfeit forms of faith. Often these counterfeit forms of faith are birthed and grounded in man's experience and not the Bible. Man's experience can fail him. However, the Word of God is true and never fails.

> *For the word of God is living and powerful, and sharper than any two-edged sword, piercing even to the division of soul and spirit, and of joints and marrow, and is a discerner of the thoughts and intents of the heart.*
>
> —-Hebrews 4:12

Faith Begins Where the Will of God is Known

Faith begins where the will of God is known. The will of God is found in the Word of God, the Bible. We just saw in Isaiah and then again in 1 Peter that it is God's will for us to be healed. Not just to be healed, but to live healed or in divine health. Your ability to walk in divine health is directly related to your revelation of who you are in Christ as a Son of God[3]. Your sonship comes with certain rights and privileges; one of which being health and prosperity. This was purchased for us. We live in the light of what we know (or for some, what we don't know). The Bible says that we are destroyed for a lack of knowledge (Hosea 4:6). Ignorance is never an excuse for operating in Bible faith and revelation. This lack of knowledge can be in various areas. The promises of God are written in the Word of God. However, if you do not appropriate the promises through faith, they will not be of any benefit to you.

My friends, faith is the key. Faith is so important to our walk that the Bible says that the "just shall live by faith" (Romans 1:17, Galatians 3:11, Hebrews 10:38). If faith is something we should be living by, it is our duty to know how it works and how it operates especially in the area of healing.

> *Now faith is the substance of things hoped for, the evidence of things not seen. 6 But without faith it is impossible to please him: for he that cometh to God must believe that he is,*

and that he is a rewarder of them that diligently seek him.

-- Hebrews 11:1, 6

This scripture discusses various elements which describe faith. It says that faith is a substance. It says that faith is the evidence of what you cannot see. It also says that faith is needed to please God. It gives us what we must believe of God to see the end result of our faith.

Let's dissect the terms used in this scripture to gain a better understanding of what the Bible is talking about. See below for the meaning of the key terms in this verse.

Key Term	Greek Definition
Faith *(pistis[4])*	Belief; persuasion; conviction based upon belief; trust; confidence; credence; assurance; fidelity – the character of one who can be relied on
Substance (hypostasis[5])	Foundation; a setting under (support); substructure; steadiness; firmness; resolution
Of things hoped for (elpizō[6])	Expect for; confidence
Evidence (elegchos[7])	Proof by which a thing is proved or tested
Impossible (adynateō[8])	Unable; not having the strength, power, or ability
Rewarder (misthapodotēs[9])	Recompense; rewarder of wages
Of them that diligently seek (ekzēteō[10])	Search out; investigate; crave; demand; require

Here we can see that faith is your belief based in the Word of God. It is a conviction based upon your beliefs. You can have faith in the positive result in line with God's Word; or you can have faith in your fear. Faith in fear is faith in the negative consequences or belief that "if God does not come through" or answer your prayer. Doubt and unbelief can short – circuit the power of God in your life.

Your expectation is a key essential to walking in Biblical faith. Faith is the confident expectation of your belief. Faith is the proof of your confident expectation based upon the Word of God. Faith gives you the proof of the unseen. The Bible further says that it is impossible to please God without it.

In the process of believing God for your healing, you must first believe that God is able and willing to heal you. That belief must be combined with expectation. Finally, corresponding actions are necessary to give life to your faith.

> *What does it profit, my brethren, if someone says he has faith but does not have works? Can faith save him? If a brother or sister is naked and destitute of daily food, and one of you says to them, "Depart in peace, be warmed and filled," but you do not give them the things which are needed for the body, what does it profit? Thus also faith by itself, if it does not have works, is dead. But someone will say, "You have faith, and I have works." Show me your faith without your works, and I will show you my faith by my works. You believe that there is one God. You do well. Even the demons believe—and tremble! 20 But do you want to know, O foolish man, that faith without works is dead?*
>
> —-James 2:14-20 NKJV

Often times well-meaning believers take this verse out of context to believe that if I do enough work towards my healing, God will see fit to heal me. Friend, you have already missed the point. Healing is a finished work. We just have to appropriate the promise in our lives. Your peace and prosperity are a finished work as well. You might ask, if it's a finished work then why am I still sick? If it's a finished work, why am I still broke? The word appropriate means to take to or for oneself; take possession of[11]. We have to take possession of the promise of healing, peace, and prosperity. How? By your faith, you must build your faith in these areas.

Your corresponding actions of faith are more of a byproduct of you acting out of what you know to be true concerning the issue. The Holy Spirit will lead and guide you in this area. He is, after all, our teacher (John 14:26). Your corresponding action should result out of a heart that believes the Word. Your corresponding action is not what needs to be done for you to believe the Word. Some say and believe in their heart, if I confess it enough, it will happen. You are not confessing the Word to get something to happen. Your confession is based in the reality that it is already done. Your confession is part of your meditation of that reality.

What you believe in your heart empowers your corresponding actions. What you believe in your heart empowers your faith. If you are really in fear and not faith, you will not have the faith result you are looking to have. At that point, you need to go back to the Word to build your faith in that area. You need to pray to God to help you and show you why it is so hard for you to believe in that area. He might show you past experiences or traumas which have created negative expectations in a certain area. The Holy Spirit might have you to deal with the consequences of that experience and forgive others or yourself. We have to be humble enough to go to God for the answers to our seemingly faith problems. The Holy Spirit knows all things and has all the answers. We must trust and rely upon Him.

Building your faith is a process. The process of faith is a life-long journey. Building faith is like building muscles. Everyone has muscles which are strengthened daily. However, if you are believing God for something specific, continue feeding yourself the Word in that area to become strong in faith and unwavering. So, when a challenge comes, your faith is ready. Don't wait for the battle, prepare beforehand. Faith must be built and encouraged in every area of our life. Our faith dismantles negative strongholds in our life that are not built in the Word of God. Bible faith requires hearing.

So then faith cometh by hearing, and hearing by the word of God.

-- Romans 10:17

Faith comes out of or arises from what you do or do not hear. You build belief systems based on what you hear. Your ears are a gate to your soul. Your soul is not who you are. We are a three part being. 1 Thessalonians 5:23 says that our whole spirit, soul, and body can be preserve. Hebrews 4:12 discusses how the Word is the divider between soul and spirit. We can biblically see that there is a definite difference between spirit, soul, and body. You are a spirit. You live in a body. You possess a soul. Feelings are the voice of the body. Reason is the voice of the soul. Conscience is the voice of your spirit.

So, the question to ask yourself is "what am I hearing?" What you are hearing has a great effect on what you produce in your life. Is what you are hearing producing the evidence of the fruit of the spirit in your life (Galatians 5:22-25) or the works of the flesh (Galatians 5:16-21)? Is what you are hearing conducive to seeing health and healing in your body? Or is it more in line with producing death, destruction, fear, and poverty? These are questions we must ask ourselves which are vital to our health, healing, and wellbeing. We are the product of what we continually hear. What we continually hear and see is what we meditate on. It is what we come into agreement with. What we come into agreement with or partner with will be evidenced in the lives we live.

For example, let's say you are in the market to buy a red car. You have done your research on this particular brand of car and you have read, seen, and listened to various information on it. Why does it seem like in your everyday walk that you see more of this particular car? Prior to wanting this car, you rarely saw it driven, but now it seems like everyone has one. You keep seeing it! My friend, that is what I am talking about. You meditated on that car. You thought about it, you read about it, you listened to various things pertaining to it. It became part of your reality. In this same way, the things we spend the most time with, meditating on via the gates of our eyes, ears, mouths, and even touch become our reality. You are the product of what you meditate on. At the end of this chapter you will find a link to receive my free guide discussing biblical meditation strategies called 3 Keys to Supernatural Revelation. If you do not hear the Word how can you believe it?

Bible Faith Requires Believing

We must believe God. The challenge of faith is believing God without seeing any physical evidence of what you believe. You believe God based on His Word and His character. His character is personified in His Word and through the life of His son Jesus. Jesus truly is the Word of God made flesh (John 1:14). You must believe without seeing the physical evidence. You must believe that God is willing and able to do what His word says.

> *Trust in the Lord with all thine heart; and lean not unto thine own understanding. In all thy ways acknowledge him, and he shall direct thy paths. Be not wise in thine own eyes: fear the Lord, and depart from evil. It shall be health to thy navel, and marrow to thy bones.*
>
> -- Proverbs 3:5-8

There is a blessing in believing and trusting God. The above scripture encourages us not to rely on our own understanding, reasoning, or thinking. This is the main reason why so many stumble in their faith. They are unable to move past what they see. They are unable to move past seeing symptoms in their bodies, they are unable to move past a negative doctor's report, and they are unable to see beyond someone else's experience. When we do this, we place out trust in them and not the Lord. We turn these things into idols and submit our mind, will, and emotions to them. We give them control. This is outside of God's will for our lives and His Word. Bible faith requires that we believe God.

> *But without faith it is impossible to please him: for he that cometh to God must believe that he is, and that he is a rewarder of them that diligently seek him.*
>
> -- Hebrews 11:6

> *Therefore I say unto you, What things soever ye desire, when ye pray, believe that ye receive them, and ye shall have them.*
>
> -- Mark 11:24

Bible Faith Requires Speaking

It has been said that the word of God or faith is "voice-activated". Your speaking what you believe is necessary to see the evidence of it in your life. Speaking can be viewed as a corresponding action of your faith.

> *For verily I say unto you, That whosoever shall say unto this mountain, Be thou removed, and be thou cast into the sea; and shall not doubt in his heart, but shall believe that those things which he saith shall come to pass; he shall have whatsoever he saith.*
>
> -- Mark 11:23

Mark 11:23 clearly says that speaking is a required element of faith that receives from God. Notice that the believing in your heart comes prior to the speaking. So often, people take this scripture to mean, "if I say it enough then I will start to believe it." This could not be further from the truth. We should be speaking from an already present reality in our souls (mind, will, and emotions). Anything other than this will not produce the intended result.

We must speak those things we believe. We were created in the image and likeness of God. He spoke things into existence. We have been given authority in this world to speak and see things and situations change and line up with the Word of God. However, this is only a reality to those who believe it and operate according to this belief.

> *(As it is written, I have made thee a father of many nations,) before him whom he believed, even God, who quickeneth the dead, and calleth those things which be not as though they were.*
>
> -- Romans 4:17

We are to mirror the actions of our Father. Here again, we see believing comes before the speaking. This scripture is in reference to Abraham who represented using Bible faith. He believed the Word of God despite what He saw in the natural (Hebrews 11:8-11; Genesis 17 & 18) concerning God's promise of blessing him with children. Our faith is realized by seeing what we believe occur. However, for our faith to work, we already should see it happening in our heart before we ever see it in the natural.

> *Do not, therefore, fling away your fearless confidence, for it carries a great and glorious compensation of reward.36 For you have need of steadfast patience and endurance, so that you may perform and fully accomplish the will of God, and thus receive and [a]carry away [and enjoy to the full] what is promised.*
>
> -- Hebrews 10:35-36 AMP

Patience is key in exercising your faith in God. In society, today, we want things to happen instantaneously. This is not always the case with God. He and His timing is sovereign. Many things in the Bible are finished works. Our healing and deliverance are finished works, bought and paid for on the cross. We were healed and delivered with the sacrifice on the cross. However, the reason why we do not walk in the fullness of the promises has to do with our appropriation of the promises. Appropriation means how we take possession of something. We can misappropriate the promises and still expect God's result. Friend, it does not work that way. In Chapter 2, we will discuss the things which we do which short-circuit our faith and cut off the promises of God from becoming a reality in our lives.

Bible Faith Requires Corresponding Actions

Our faith requires corresponding actions. As we just discussed, speaking can be viewed as a corresponding action of your faith. Your speaking can come in the form of declarations of what you know to be true, praise and worship of God... really anything coming out of your mouth as a testament of what you believe. Your corresponding actions entail obeying, acting, and doing. The Bible describes corresponding actions as "works".

> *Even so faith, if it hath not works, is dead, being alone.*

> --James 2:17

If your faith does not have works, the Bible says it is the same as your faith being dead or inoperative and ineffective. The corresponding actions of your faith are determined by you and God. What does your acting in faith look like? What would you be doing? Consider these things, and obey what God tells you to do.

A special note of clarification is needed here. God will not tell you to do anything that would be hurtful to you. That is not the nature and character of God. Alongside of faith, we must operate in wisdom. Your corresponding actions might be uncomfortable to your flesh, but they will not hurt you. For example, you throw away your medication without doctor verification could be hurtful to you. If you feel that you do not need your meds prayerfully consider it and let the doctor confirm what you believe to be true in your heart via natural medical tests.

Doctors and medicine can be seen as God's grace and mercy until we appropriate His promises in our lives. Do not stop what God is trying to do in your life by operating in foolishness by rejecting doctors and modern medicine. God can partner with your doctor and modern medicine to cause health to break forth in your body. In all things, we must consider and acknowledge God. We must follow His leading and guidance.

In my own life with my husband, we had to make this choice. As you know from reading the beginning of this book. My husband and I partnered with doctors and modern medicine to see the total restoration of his body. When my husband, Royce's, kidney function was at 3% he did not want to undergo kidney dialysis treatment. He believed that this was an act of his faith. He wanted God to just give him the creative miracle of new kidneys. God can do this, however, after much prayer, this did not happen. Royce counseled with our pastor and underwent treatment. Royce wanted God to heal him in a certain way. His restoration came through the help of modern medicine. There is a lot more to this story and can be read in the introduction of this book. In the end, we partnered with medicine and was led by the Holy Spirit in all our decisions. We saw the hand of God moving within the medical treatment Royce was receiving. We had to believe God through the treatments because many things can go wrong. Praise God that Royce thrived with the treatments and eventually received a new kidney and pancreas via a transplant. If we had not followed the Holy Spirit and succumbed to fear, Royce might not be here today.

Many times, we feel like we are in faith, but we are really in what is called mental assent. Mental assent was first discussed by theologian John Wesley in the 1700's. Mental assent means that you believe the word in your head mentally, but you do not truly believe it in your heart. You agree with the Word in your head, but do not truly think it will work on your behalf. You agree that God exists and that His word is true. You are virtually just hoping something happens and not believing by faith. There is one major difference between hope and faith, and that difference is action. Faith acts (James 2:14). You can have hope by just thinking that something can happen. However, faith says that whatever you are believing for is yours and you add corresponding actions to your hope turning it into faith.

Healing is God's best for your life. God desires that you live in divine health. This comes through knowing that God loves you and want the absolute best for you. He wants you to prosper in all things. He wants you to live a full and victorious life. He wants you healthy enough to complete the purpose He has created you for before the foundation of this Earth. We have a real enemy that wants death and destruction for the people of God. He wants to see you destroyed because he hates God. Let's not submit to the plan of the enemy ignorance and fear. Let's abide close to the Father, be led by Him and experience the life He sent His son to Earth to suffer and die for so that we may live!

Activation Prayer

God, I come to you in the name of Jesus. Thank you for showing me your heart concerning healing. I believe that healing is for me right now. I accept your love and guidance in this area. I commit to submit to your instruction and wisdom. Please send divine connections my way to help encourage me in my faith. Thank you for your life resident in my body effecting a healing and a cure. Thank you for revelation knowledge and grace to win. In Jesus name I pray, Amen.

Next Steps

1. Examine your actions. Have you been acting in faith? In your journal, list the areas where you are believing God. Are you in faith concerning these things?

2. Examine your thoughts. Are you in fear concerning what you are believing God for?

3. If you discover you are not in faith yet, find scriptures to encourage you in your faith. Use the keys in the 3 Keys to Supernatural Revelations (downloadable in book bonuses on www.drandreaihart.com) to meditate on these truths.

4. Find people who believe like you and ask them to stand in faith with you. Tell them what you are believing God for and share with them the scriptures you are standing on.

Prescription for Divine Health: The Doctor is In

If you are having symptoms in your body, see a doctor to get them checked out. Do not be in fear of receiving a diagnosis. Jesus has given us His name which is above every name. Every sickness and disease must bow to the name of Jesus! Annually see your doctor for your physical. Get bloodwork done and believe God to walk in divine health. Go to our website to see what annual visits you should be having throughout the year based on your age. Let's be people of wisdom and prudence when it comes to our health. We only get one body on this Earth. Let's take care of it the best we can. Let's allow God to put His "super" on our "natural"!

CHAPTER 2

I Don't Have Enough Faith to be Healed

WHEN FACED WITH SEEMINGLY impossible circumstances and God seems far away or not intervening; we often come up with excuses as to why things are not going the way we believe. We develop reasons as to why God is not working. One of these excuses or reasonings is that "I do not have enough faith" to receive my healing. Have you ever thought that when you did not receive the promise from God? We know there is nothing wrong with God, therefore there must be something wrong with me...or else God would have moved when I asked Him to!

Friend, we have to know that sometimes when situations do not go our way after we have to pray for a certain outcome, there could be other things at work short-circuiting the power of God. This can especially be the case when dealing with another person. God will not overrule a person's will. He gives us free will for a reason. He wants us to be able to choose. We can pray well-meaning prayers, but God does not control us like robots. Many times, we come into agreement with Satan and as a result we have the consequences of following him.

At times when we do not receive what we want from God, it is a "surrender" issue not a faith issue. Do not believe the lie of the devil. You have enough faith to be healed. Why? You have God's capacity for faith.

You Have God's Capacity of Faith

> *And Jesus, replying, said to them, Have faith in God [constantly]. Truly I tell you, whoever says to this mountain, Be lifted up and thrown into the sea! and does not doubt at all in his heart but believes that what he says will take place, it will be done for him. For this reason I am telling you, whatever you ask for in prayer, believe (trust and be confident) that it is granted to you, and you will [get it].*

-- Mark 11:22-24 AMP

The first line of the scripture literally means "have the faith of God". Jesus operated using God's faith. He also told the disciples to operate with this faith. God would not tell you to do something without giving you the ability to do it! You have God's capacity for faith. You have God's spirit, the Holy Spirit, residing on the inside of you. You have God's word and God's spirit. Therefore, you can produce God's results. The reality of this truth is that using God's faith yields God's results! Galatians 2:20 also admonishes us to use God's faith and not our own natural human faith. Using natural human faith leads to faith failure almost 100% of the time.

> *I am crucified with Christ: nevertheless I live; yet not I, but Christ liveth in me: and the life which I now live in the flesh I live by the faith of the Son of God, who loved me, and gave himself for me.*
>
> -- Galatians 2:20

We are to live by the faith of God. The Bible also says over and over again that the just shall live by faith (Habakkuk 2:4, Rom.

1:17, Gal. 3:11, Heb. 10:38). We are given God's capacity to believe because we have the spirit of God living big on the inside of us. The Bible goes as far as saying that we are "one spirit" with Christ (1 Cor. 6:17). The Living Bible says, " But if you give yourself to the Lord, you and Christ are joined together as one person." The reality of this truth enables you to operate and have faith victories every time! Healing was bought and paid for us over 2000 years ago with Jesus's death on the cross and assention into heaven. We cannot do any more for our healing then what already has been done. We just need to receive it!

What Stops Your Faith from Working?

Your faith is designed to work. This is how God created it. By nature, it is designed to effectively work every time. If this was not so, why would Jesus tell us that the "just shall live by faith" (Hebrews 10:38). To live by something, it needs to be able to work every time. Your faith has the ability to work every time you attempt to use it. Your faith is simply your belief based on the evidence of the Word of God. In Chapter 1, we went through the biblical definition of faith extensively. Review it if you need a refresher.

However, there are other things we let prohibit our faith from working effectively. There are three main issues that I will discuss. We can look at the disciples as an example for the first hindrance to our faith, not using our faith in the proper manner. The account of Jesus taming the wind and seas can be found in the gospels of Mark, Matthew, and Luke (Mark 4:35-41; Matthew 8:23-27; Luke 8:22-25). We will look at Mark's account.

Example #1 Jesus in the Storm

> *And the same day, when the even was come, he saith unto them, Let us pass over unto the other side. And when they had sent away the multitude, they took him even as he was in*

the ship. And there were also with him other little ships. And there arose a great storm of wind, and the waves beat into the ship, so that it was now full. And he was in the hinder part of the ship, asleep on a pillow: and they awake him, and say unto him, Master, carest thou not that we perish? And he arose, and rebuked the wind, and said unto the sea, Peace, be still. And the wind ceased, and there was a great calm. And he said unto them, Why are ye so fearful? how is it that ye have no faith? And they feared exceedingly, and said one to another, What manner of man is this, that even the wind and the sea obey him?

-- Mark 4:35-41

We see here Jesus used His faith to cause the wind and sea to be calm. He admonished the disciples for their fear. He corrected them for not using their faith effectively. He asked them "how is it you have no faith?" Coming into agreement and acting out of fear in Jesus's mind was like not even having faith at all. When it comes to faith, if you are in fear that is your number one indicator that you are not in faith. Fear and faith cannot abide with one another. If your actions are based in fear, you are NOT in faith. You will not receive what you are believing for from God.

In Matthew's account of this story, Jesus describes the disciples as having little faith in chapter 8. He says, "...Why are ye so fearful, O ye of little faith?" In Luke's account, Jesus asked "Where is your faith?" We can see through these three accounts that faith is there, however, fear hindered faith's function. The disciples came into agreement with fear when they looked at their circumstances. They looked at the wind and waves.

When thinking about your healing, what are you looking at? Are you looking at the symptoms, doctors report, or your emotions? What is causing you to fear? Ask yourself these questions and you will be able to pinpoint if you are truly in faith or in fear. This could be the reason you are not receiving from God. Take an inventory of every area of your life and make the appropriate adjustments to evict the fear in those areas.

Example #2 Peter Walking on the Water

And straightway Jesus constrained his disciples to get into a ship, and to go before him unto the other side, while he sent the multitudes away.²³ And when he had sent the multitudes away, he went up into a mountain apart to pray: and when the evening was come, he was there alone. But the ship was now in the midst of the sea, tossed with waves: for the wind was contrary. And in the fourth watch of the night Jesus went unto them, walking on the sea. And when the disciples saw him walking on the sea, they were troubled, saying, It is a spirit; and they cried out for fear. But straightway Jesus spake unto them, saying, Be of good cheer; it is I; be not afraid. And Peter answered him and said, Lord, if it be thou, bid me come unto thee on the water. And he said, Come. And when Peter was come down out of the ship, he walked on the water, to go to Jesus. But when he saw the wind boisterous, he was afraid; and beginning to sink, he cried, saying, Lord, save me. And immediately Jesus stretched forth his hand, and caught him, and said unto him, O thou of little faith, wherefore didst thou doubt? And when they were come into the ship, the wind ceased. Then they that were in the ship came and worshipped him, saying, Of a truth thou art the Son of God. And when they were gone over, they came into the land of Gennesaret.

-- Matthew 14:22-34

In this story, Jesus was walking on the water. Peter walked on the water simply on Jesus's word "come". In the same way, we can use our faith and walk on the words of Jesus when in a situation that seems impossible. What we see from this story is that at the moment Peter took His focus off Jesus and focused on the situation and negative circumstances, he became distracted and began to sink. In the same way, when using our faith, when we lose focus and get distracted, our faith wavers, and we do not receive what we are believing. Doubt set in with Peter when he began looking at the circumstances. In a similar fashion, when we begin to focus on our symptoms, sickness, and disease doubt can set in and cause our faith to waver. This wavering faith will cause us to miss out on what we are believing for God to do.

Where is Your Faith?

How do you think faith is seen? How is it recognized? You can know someone is in faith based upon their actions. Jesus was able to see an individual faith. We see an example of this in the Word in the story of the man who was sick with palsy (Luke 5:17-25). In this story, men were looking to bring an invalid who was paralyzed to Jesus to be healed. However, it was crowded where Jesus was teaching. These men believed that Jesus was able to heal this man so much that they went on the roof, removed the tiles and lowered him to Jesus. They had crazy faith! They were not worried about what they looked like to others. These people were desperate. Everyone that saw that, saw their faith. They were serious and knew Jesus could heal their friend. It says that when he saw their faith, he commanded the man to get up and walk. This man was healed instantly.

Can Your Faith be Seen?

Can your faith be seen by others? This is an essential component of active effectual faith. Faith requires corresponding actions. Otherwise it is just hope. This might be a key to why you may not be receiving from God.

So also faith, if it does not have works (deeds and actions of obedience to back it up), by itself is destitute of power (inoperative, dead). But someone will say [to you then], You [say you] have faith, and I have [good] works. Now you show me your [alleged] faith apart from any [good] works [if you can], and I by [good] works [of obedience] will show you my faith. You believe that God is one; you do well. So do the demons believe and shudder [in terror and horror such as [a] make a man's hair stand on end and contract the surface of his skin]! Are you willing to be shown [proof], you foolish (unproductive, spiritually deficient) fellow, that faith apart from [good] works is inactive and ineffective and worthless?

-- James 2:17-20 AMPC

People think they are in faith; however, their actions are not there, or their actions are motivated by fear. Corresponding actions are actions that are *NOT* rooted in fear or presumption. The corresponding actions of faith are individualistic. You must seek God to ask Him what corresponding actions would illustrate your faith. This should come naturally to you. We do not have to be "super-spiritual" about it. Look into your heart and let the Holy Spirit lead you. This might not be the same for everyone. God knows where you are in your faith walk. He just wants you to take at least one baby step towards Him!

Another example of faith in action is with the Centurion servant found in Matthew Chapter 8. This is another case of someone sick with palsy or paralyzed.

Jesus said, "I will come and heal him." [8] But the officer said, "Lord, I am not worthy to have you come into my home. Just say the word from where you are, and my servant will be healed. I know this because I am under the authority of my superior officers, and I have authority over my soldiers. I only need to say, 'Go,' and they go, or 'Come,' and they come. And if I say to my slaves, 'Do this,' they do it." [10] When Jesus heard this, he was amazed. Turning to those who were following him, he said, "I tell you the truth, I haven't seen faith like this in all Israel!"

-- Matthew 8:7-10 NLT

In this story, we can see that Jesus judged this man's faith for his servant based on his actions. In Jesus's estimation, this man had great faith. The Centurion's faith was grounded in his revelation of authority. He understood the authority that Jesus carried as the Son of God. He understood Jesus's authority over sickness and disease. He understood that sickness and disease was Jesus's servant. It had to obey Him. Due to the Centurion's revelation, he did not even require that Jesus physically come to minister to his servant. He knew Jesus's word alone would set things in motion and his servant would be healed. Jesus recognized this man's faith in his actions to seek him out, just for a word. The greatness in this man's faith was demonstrated in how he used his faith. He believed and acted before he saw anything.

Your Faith Requires Endurance

Sometimes when we are believing God, we give up too easily. When we do not see what we prayed for on our time schedule, we give up on our faith in God and attempt to work in our own strength and power for the thing we were believing God. Hebrews chapter 11 is often called the "faith hall of fame" it discusses the faith of Abraham and Sarah. They were given a promise from God and continued in faith. They died not physically seeing all that God had promised them.

These all died in faith, not having received the promises, but having seen them afar off, and were persuaded of them, and embraced them, and confessed that they were strangers and pilgrims on the earth.

-- Hebrews 11:13

Abraham and Sarah received much from God. However, they did not see all that God promised them in their lifetime on this Earth and that's okay. The Bible describes our life as a believer as a race. This race is not a sprint, but a marathon. We must be content in the journey and not try to operate outside of Christ's timing. Paul is the Bible's greatest example of this.

> *Save that the Holy Ghost witnesseth in every city, saying that bonds and afflictions abide me. But none of these things move me, neither count I my life dear unto myself, so that I might finish my course with joy, and the ministry, which I have received of the Lord Jesus, to testify the gospel of the grace of God.*
>
> -- Acts 20:23-24

This is the attitude we must have as believers. The "things" which Paul was referring to in this scripture can be found in 2 Corinthians 11:22-27. He battled throughout his whole ministry. He experienced great persecution from being beaten, jailed, robbed, and the list goes on.

Paul did not give up. He had a promise and mission from God. He was compelled to pursue his purpose when he was attacked, and things did not seem easy. In the same way, healing is a promise from God. The devil will try to get you to reject what God has promised through fear and worry. However, we must not back down and hold onto the promises of God. We should strive to have the same testimony of Paul.

> *I have fought a good fight, I have finished my course, I have kept the faith: Henceforth there is laid up for me a crown of righteousness, which the Lord, the righteous judge, shall give me at that day: and not to me only, but unto all them also that love his appearing.*
>
> -- 2 Timothy 4:7-8

Satan wants to keep you sick and diseased, so you will not be able to effectively complete the call and purposes of God for your life. Attacking you with sickness and disease is his way of attacking God since you are God's prized possession. Satan wants to destroy the plans of God by any means necessary. He wants to steal from us, kill us, and destroy us (John 10:10).

You have to know what belongs to you as a member of the family of God and be determined to receive and possess all of it. You must be persistent with "bulldog" faith to receive all of the promises of God despite what you see going on inside or around you. The woman with the issue of blood in Mark 5 exhibited this kind of endurance and persistence.

> *And a certain woman, which had an issue of blood twelve years, And had suffered many things of many physicians, and had spent all that she had, and was nothing bettered, but rather grew worse, When she had heard of Jesus, came in the press behind, and touched his garment. For she said, If I may touch but his clothes, I shall be whole. And straightway the fountain of her blood was dried up; and she felt in her body that she was healed of that plague. And Jesus, immediately knowing in himself that virtue had gone out of him, turned him about in the press, and said, Who touched my clothes? And his disciples said unto him, Thou seest the multitude thronging thee, and sayest thou, Who touched me? And he looked round about to see her that had done this thing. But the woman fearing and trembling, knowing what was done in her, came and fell down before him, and told him all the truth. And he said unto her, Daughter, thy faith hath made thee whole; go in peace, and be whole of thy plague.*

> -- Mark 5:25-34

We can see from this story that this woman had endurance. She had seen many physicians trying to find relief for her ailment. So much so, she was bankrupt! Jesus was her last hope. She pressed her way to receive from Jesus. As a woman with this type of problem, during Jewish times, she was considered ceremonially unclean (Lev.15:19-30). She was not even supposed to be in public because the Jews believed she was defiled, and everything she touched would be defiled. However, she forsook all and operated in faith to receive from Jesus. She was persistent in her faith and confession. She said that once she touched Jesus, she was going to be made completely whole.

What is your confession of faith? What are your corresponding actions of faith? This woman was acting on her faith. God saw her faith, and she received from God instantaneously. She had so much against her. She was dealing with a long – term illness, medical science of that day could not help her. She had no money. She was an outcast. She had no support or help. Yet she moved based on what she had heard about Jesus! We need to operate in the same way. We have all the words of Jesus in the Bible, we have the Holy Spirit, and the ability to have a relationship with the Father. We have so many more reasons to believe than she might have had. Yet she still was determined, demonstrated endurance, and received from God. So, what is stopping you from receiving?

Activation Prayer

Father, I repent for not believing your promises concerning (*insert area(s) where you have had issues believing God*). Right now, I commit to develop my faith in the Word of God. Please help me and give me wisdom, knowledge, understand, and revelation of your promises. Help me to understand your faith and show me what things I can do to improve in my faith walk. I renounce fear and all things that come with it. I choose to operate in faith. I thank you for a deeper understanding of your love for me. I choose to listen to the voice of the Holy Spirit and be obedient to you at all times. Thank you for your strength to fulfill your purposes in my life. In Jesus's name, Amen.

Next Steps

1. Decide to read, study, and meditate in the Word of God. Go to www.drandreaihart.com for resources to help.

2. Schedule a daily time to fellowship with God through prayer and meditating His word. Use your journal to write down the things God speaks to your heart and any scriptures you are meditating on.

3. Ask God to connect you with an accountability partner who will stand in faith with you and encourage you throughout your faith walk. If you do not have a church, pray that the Lord will direct you to a body of like-minded believers for you to fellowship.

4. Connect with me via the web at www.drandreaihart.com and let me know how you are doing. Please leave any prayer requests that we can stand in faith with you.

Prescription for Divine Health: Give Gratitude

Write down the words, "family", "friends", "me", "work", "church/ spirituality", and "community" on separate pages of your journal. Each of these pages is the beginning of your gratitude section of your journal. At times, we can tend to focus on the negative or what we don't have. This affects your mental health and outlook on life. Research has shown that having a gratitude journal is connected to improved well-being, mental health, and happiness. Realizing who and what you are grateful for builds faith and expectation to God. It also gives you renewed hope. On each page daily think of at least one thing you are thankful for. You can write more than that, but this is just a start. You can go as far as you need to, add additional areas, etc. Make this activity your own!

CHAPTER 3

ROOT SYSTEMS

WE HAVE TO EXAMINE ourselves to receive clues to why we act the way we do. This can be essential when you are trying to figure out why certain things have occurred certain ways in your life. This is of the utmost importance when determining the results of your faith. In the last chapter, we discussed one of the main reasoning or excuses someone might use when believing God for healing and not seeing it as a reality in their lives. The belief that you do not have enough faith is the most common reason for not receiving healing from God. We dismantled this reasoning in Chapter 2.

However, we also must determine carefully, what is our faith in? At face value, this seems to be a simple question. The most likely answer for the average Christian would be that my faith in in Jesus! To that my response would be, what else is your faith in? Is your faith in your past experiences? Is your faith in your past "faith failures"? Is your faith in your doctor? These are some of the questions we must ask ourselves when we are attempting to "troubleshoot" why we have not received from God. God is always willing and waiting to see His perfect will as a reality in our lives.

Troubleshooting Your Faith

Faith always requires our belief in something. Our belief starts as hope. We need some type of evidence for our hope to transform it into faith. Examine why you believe what you believe. What things have you told yourself to justify your experience with believing God for things and not seeing them occur? For example, do you believe that you can never move from a certain class in life? No one in your family has ever been a millionaire, so you will never believe for that level of wealth. We must take these experiences and ask ourselves is the experience of not having enough or living in poverty preventing me from believing God? Is this mental picture holding my faith back? Has this reality become a stronghold in my life? Have repeated negative experiences in this area built a fortress in my mind and thoughts preventing me from effectively believing God? We must have real conversations with ourselves and ask the hard questions. Asking the hard questions causes us to "troubleshoot" our belief systems. What belief systems do you have established in your heart based on experiences?

What are the roots of your beliefs?

When we take a careful look at our belief systems, it provides clues to the realities we experience in our lives. How we think directly affects the decisions we make. We are triune or three-part beings. Your thoughts are processed in your soulish realm. Our goal is to let our spirits be our guide. We are spirits. We live in a body and we possess a soul. Our soul is made up of our mind, will, and emotions. Feelings are the voice of the body. Reason is the voice of the soul. Conscience is the voice of our spirits (1 Thess. 5:23; Hebrews 4:12).

Our souls are impacted by experiences that we go through, good or bad. These experiences help to formulate our belief systems. It is God's will for us to be able to process these experiences with His help and His Word. Good and bad experiences are part of life. It is how we process these experiences which determines the affect that they have on our souls. Often traumatic experiences impact our souls so significantly that it affects our interpretation of the world around us. The effects of these traumatic experiences influence our decision-making, our coping skills, and at times our personalities.

Strongholds are a firmly fortified set of values or beliefs that has been established in the mind and/or emotions often triggered by a circumstances, experiences, or events. We have to recognize the negative strongholds that exist that are outside of God's Word and proceed to dismantle these thoughts and reasonings systematically. This is something that must be done on purpose. Negative strongholds are based on lies and deception of the enemy. We must on purpose counteract and reject his thoughts and reasonings. They are not your thoughts. They are manufactured by the enemy.

> *For though, we walk in the flesh, we do not war according to the flesh. For the weapons of our warfare are not carnal but mighty in God for pulling down strongholds, casting down arguments (imaginations) and every high thing that exalts itself against the knowledge of God, bringing every thought into captivity to the obedience of Christ,*
>
> -- 2 Corinthians 10:3-5 NKJV

> *To counteract the thoughts of the enemy we must first realize which thoughts are ours and which thoughts are the enemy. This can only be done with the Word of God. For the word of God is alive and powerful. It is sharper than the sharpest two-edged sword, cutting between soul and spirit, between joint and marrow. It exposes our innermost thoughts and desires. Nothing in all creation is hidden from God. Everything is naked and exposed before his eyes, and he is the one to whom we are accountable.*
>
> -- Hebrews 4:12-13 NLT

The Word of God exposes the lies of the enemy. The Word of God gives us a biblical world-view. It is the Word of God which tells us how to think. It gives us God's mind. It gives us the mind of Christ if we choose to renew our minds to its truths (1 Cor. 2:16; Romans 12:1-2). If we meditate on the Word according to Joshua 1:8 our lives will be changed.

In society today, the New Age movement, has hijacked the term meditation and has turned it into something directed to pursue self-realization and their form of peace based in secular practices outside of Jesus. New Age meditation and mysticism will lead you down the path to hosting and forming agreements with demonic spirits. It is an open door to the satanic in your life. True meditation originated in the Bible. Biblical meditation involves the Word of God and leads to Godly mind renewal (Romans 12:1).

Practicing Biblical Meditation

The word meditate occurs fourteen times in the bible. First in Genesis with Isaac but then again in Joshua. The bible continues to discuss the great benefits of meditating the word of God from the Old to the New Testaments (Gen. 24:63; Josh. 1:8; Psalms 1:2; Psalms 63:6; Psalms 77:12; Psalms 119:15,23,48,78,148; Psalms 143:5; 1 Timothy 4:15). The word meditate means to murmur or mutter and gives the implication of pondering 1. According to the scripture, we are to speak the Word of God to ourselves and think about it day and night. This practice will build God's revelation in our life. We will be building Godly strongholds and uprooting negative belief systems. If you have not already gone to http://bit.ly/godstillhealsbonus to get your free resource – "3 Keys to Supernatural Revelation Guide," go there now and receive life changing information on renewing your mind.

Examining Your Thoughts and Belief Systems

The way in which we think is of great importance to how and why we believe the way we do. One of the ways that we comprehend and interpret life is through our memories. Our memories are comprised of stories. Time periods and other objects are "attached" to these memories. Right now, you can probably recollect a memory from your past. In that memory, certain items remind you of that moment in time. These items, experiences, people, and things can cause you to think of that memory.

Our brain works in a way that when we process information, we attempt to link similar thoughts and memories together. We tend to remember things which remind us of something familiar or relate to an experience we have had before. This is how we create something called a schema. "A schema is a cognitive framework or concept that helps organize and interpret information. Schemas can be useful because they allow us to take shortcuts in interpreting the vast amount of information that is available in our environment. However, these mental frameworks also cause us to exclude pertinent information to focus instead only on things that confirm our pre-existing beliefs and ideas. Schemas can contribute to stereotypes and make it difficult to retain new information that does not conform to our established ideas about the world."[2,3,4]

Psychological theorist, Jean Piaget, first termed this relationship between an individual's experience and their formation of intellect and cognitive development. Piaget also discovered that once these schemas are formed they are not "set in stone". The process of adjusting or changing your schemas is called assimilation or accommodation. "In assimilation, new information is incorporated into pre-existing schemas. In accommodation, existing schemas might be altered or new schemas might be formed as a person learns new information and has new experiences."[2,3,4] At times individuals believe so much in their pre-existing schemas that they are unwilling to change them when new information is given which contradicts them. This results in individuals interpreting everything in light of their existing schemas.

Therefore, I urge you, brothers and sisters, by the mercies of God, to present your bodies [dedicating all of yourselves, set apart] as a living sacrifice, holy and well-pleasing to God, which is your rational (logical, intelligent) act of worship. And do not be conformed to this world [any longer with its superficial values and customs], but be transformed and progressively changed [as you mature spiritually] by the renewing of your mind [focusing on godly values and ethical attitudes], so that you may prove [for yourselves] what the will of God is, that which is good and acceptable and perfect [in His plan and purpose for you].

-- Romans 12:1-2 AMP

The Bible says that the Word is strong enough to uproot your existing thoughts, patterns, and ways developed through living in this world. One of my favorite scriptures, Hebrews 4:12 says that the Word of God is quick and powerful. It is able to rightly divide that which is spirit and that which comes out of your own mind, will, and emotions. Therefore, the Word of God is more than able to uproot pre-existing schemas which are not in line with the Bible. We just have to spend time meditating in the Word of God to let it transform us more and more. In Romans 12:2 the Greek Word for "conform" is syschēmatizō. It means to conform one's self (i.e. one's mind and character) to another's pattern, (fashion one's self according to), to fashion alike, i.e. conform to the same pattern. It is also very interesting to see that this is the Greek word in which our word schema is derived from![6] The Greek word for "transform" is *metamorphoo* it means to change into another form; transfigure.[7] A natural example of this type of change is of a caterpillar transforming into a butterfly.

The Word of God changes us radically. We just have to yield to the change that God can do in our lives. The Contemporary English version of the Bible says,

Anyone who belongs to Christ is a new person. The past is forgotten, and everything is new.

-- 1 Corinthians 5:17 CEV

God can and will by the power of the Holy Spirit change our old sinful schemas. Often, we accept experiences as doctrine. What we believe about God should be based on the Bible NOT only our experiences. If your experiences cannot be justified by the Word of God throw them out and do not base your actions on them. True Bible faith believes the Word despite what our circumstances say. We declare the Word over our circumstances until the circumstances conform to the Word.

For example, if you have pain in your body and you know that the Word of God says in 1 Peter 2:24 (DARBY) who himself bore our sins in his body on the tree, in order that, being dead to sins, we may live to righteousness: by whose stripes ye have been healed. You need to speak that scripture to the circumstance (the pain in your body). Your body has no choice but to line up. You might have to do this over and over, but your body will follow suit (Romans 4:17). This is part of your corresponding action to your faith. Meditating on this Word will cause it to become real to you in your heart and you are guaranteed to see the manifestation of this truth in your life. This is the life of faith. The Bible says that we are to live by faith (Hebrews 10:38, Galatians 3:11, Romans 1:17, Habakkuk 2:4). In my opinion, this is one of the chief ways that we that live and exercise our faith.

What are your schemas?

What are your schemas? Where did they come from? These are questions that we must ask ourselves to thoroughly analyze our experiences. At times, we need emotional healing or inner healing from our past hurts and pains caused by others or even ourselves. Often when we have been deeply hurt by someone that close to us or someone that we hold in high esteem in our younger years. It bruises our souls.

We must take a hard look at our lives. In what areas do you not reflect Christ? In what areas of your personality is Christ's fruit of the Spirit not evident? These are areas we need to work on. These are areas that need healing. Ask the Lord to show you what experiences or traumas caused you to develop certain personality traits that are outside of the fruit of the spirit. If this is a difficult task, ask a trusted friend or Christian counselor to help you in this activity.

> *But the Holy Spirit produces this kind of fruit in our lives: love, joy, peace, patience, kindness, goodness, faithfulness, gentleness, and self-control. There is no law against these things! Those who belong to Christ Jesus have nailed the passions and desires of their sinful nature to his cross and crucified them there. Since we are living by the Spirit, let us follow the Spirit's leading in every part of our lives.*

> -- Galatians 5:22-25 NLT

We must be real with ourselves for true healing to result. You cannot receive total and complete restorative healing and transformation for that which you will not confront. We must confront those things and tendencies which are not like God. We must come out of agreement with thoughts and activities which are not in agreement with the Word of God. Healing is included in the salvation package. God did not look at our sins and judge if we were worthy to receive his healing. He provided it in the person of Jesus while we were yet sinners. However, to live in a place of divine health, we must commit to living a victorious life that is grounded in the Word of God. The Word is a keeper of our souls.

> *Christ himself carried our sins in his body to the cross, so that we might die to sin and live for righteousness. It is by his wounds that you have been healed. You were like sheep that*

had lost their way, but now you have been brought back to follow the Shepherd and Keeper of your souls.

-- 1 Peter 2:24-25 GNB

Overcoming Your Past Traumatic Experiences

If God shows you trauma in your past which has shaped your current reality, God will give you the grace and ability to confront and address these issues. At the end of this chapter and on my website, there are additional resources to help you with this. The simple definition of trauma is an experience(s) which causes significant distress or disturbance to an individual. This experience often has long term effects on a person's mind, will, and emotions (soul). In a majority of cases, this experience is associated with a person, place, or thing which holds significance and authority in an individual's life. This is often seen in individuals with a stressful childhood as a result of their family structure or dysfunction. Often without proper coping skills and resiliency frameworks in place, these experiences can affect and shape a person's soul. These experiences can also become an open door for sickness, disease, and demonic activity in a person's life.

Trauma can be evidenced by traumatic pictures (painful memories) and ungodly beliefs in a person's heart that are not true. These beliefs drive that person's life. Trauma is like the infection in the wound. Trauma can be either emotional, physical, or both. A person's soul can be tied to the traumatic experience. This means that a person's mind, will, and emotions can be intertwined with the traumatic experience. This intertwining of the thoughts and memories of the trauma impacts our actions. It can cause us to build walls around our souls to protect them from being hurt and wounded again. At times our reaction to the traumatic experience perverts or mutates our identity. This is especially important if the trauma happened during our formative years in childhood or young adulthood. At times with severe trauma, people experience a pause in their emotional growth at the point of the trauma. When confronted with certain situations or triggers, people will regress to the age which they were when the trauma occurred. For example, if the trauma was at 8 years old, the person will respond the same way he/she did when they were 8 years old.

Jesus is the anchor to our souls. He died for every trauma that we have or will experience (Isaiah 53: 4-5). Your deliverance must come through Him. Many times, spirits of infirmity can attach to traumatic soul ties or experiences. Prayer must take place to displace and root out the enemy's stronghold in our lives in areas of trauma. Many times, when inner healing and deliverance occurs to counteract trauma, physical healing takes place. Unaddressed or unhealed trauma may be seen in your personality. You may have anger or rage issues, rejection, co-dependency, self-worth or self-esteem issues, among other things. In the writing of this book, I am not able to dissect this subject in depth. Please connect via the contact information found in the back of this book to be notified of additional resources on this subject.

The Bible speaks of trauma in the story of the good Samaritan found in Luke 10:25-37. This story chronicles the story of a traveler who was abused and attached by thieves. These thieves attacked him and took his clothing and wounded him. The thieves left this traveler for dead. Three others passed this man on the road, a priest, Levite, and a Samaritan. The priest and the Levite saw the man and passed on the other side. The Samaritan was the only one who stopped and helped the wounded man.

> *But a Samaritan (foreigner), who was traveling, came upon him; and when he saw him, he was deeply moved with compassion [for him], and went to him and bandaged up his wounds, pouring oil and wine on them [to sooth and disinfect the injuries]; and he put him on his own pack-animal, and brought him to an inn and took care of him. On the next day*

> *he took out two denarii (two days' wages) and gave them to the innkeeper, and said, 'Take care of him; and whatever more you spend, I will repay you when I return.'*

-- Luke 10:33-35 AMP

In this story, the road from Jerusalem to Jericho was known as a dangerous road to travel in Biblical times due to having a reputation of being frequented by robbers. In this scripture, two different Greek words are used for the word wound in verses 30 and 34. In verse 30 the word "wound" is translated as stripe. However, in verse 34 the word wound is translated as "trauma". What changed from verse 30 to 34? The word trauma in verse 34 gives the connotation of multiple stripes/wounds. Perhaps the rejection of the priest and Levite affected the man more than we know. The point is that it began as just a wound and then turned in to trauma as a result of repeated wounding. This man experienced physical pain. However, emotionally, he most likely felt rejection, shame, fear, betrayal, violation, abandonment, and grief (loss). This came at the hand of the robbers and at the hands of the Levite and priest. The Samaritan demonstrated compassion and essentially paid the price for this man's restoration expecting nothing in return.

Jesus did the same for us. We can look at the Samaritan as a symbol of the love and compassion that Jesus demonstrated to us when He died for us. Jesus continues to demonstrate His love and compassion to us daily. Jesus provided the cure for sickness, disease, and trauma. We must accept it by faith. He has already provided for us. Let the love of God heal you of past hurt, pain, and trauma. Why not forgive the person or persons who played a part in causing you hurt and pain? Your healing is found in your forgiveness. Forgive those who have hurt you, despite what they did. Give up your right for vengeance. God will deal with those individuals. However, your inability to forgive has caused an open door for the enemy to attack you in your body and soul. If forgiveness is difficult, as the Holy Spirit for strength, help and guidance.

In your heart, go back to that place and time of trauma. Jesus was right there with you. Ask God to show you where Jesus was when you were going through the pain, hurt, and trauma. He was always there. He will always be there to bind up your wounds and provide restoration to you heat, mind, will, and emotions. Decide today to trust Him and allow Him to restore you.

Activation Prayer

Father, give me strength to be able to examine my life, especially the painful times when I have felt alone and abandoned. Help me to identify the roots of my pain and any emotional hurt which might still exist in my heart. I forgive those who have caused this pain to me. I give them to you. I accept your love, Father. I accept your restoration in these areas. I commit to follow you and I accept your love for me even during the hard times when I have felt alone. Thank you for always loving and caring for me. Thank you for always being there. In Jesus' name, Amen.

Next Steps

1. Spend some quiet time with God. Ask the Lord to show you your heart. What have you been putting your faith in regarding your healing? What pain or trauma have you come into agreement with? Pay attention to what God shows you. He might show you a picture on the screen of your mind or speak something to your heart. Write what He shows you in your journal.

2. Depending on what God shows you, find scriptures to study and meditate on in those areas. For example, if he showed you that you were in fear, find scriptures and passages which demonstrate God's love for you.

3. Expect change to occur in your situation. Reject having a failure mindset or mentality. Stand in your faith. At the time

you prayed, God answered (Mark 11:24-25). Thank God now and continue to thank Him regardless of what you see.

Prescription for Divine Health: Practice Focus

Practice focus. Focus on what you are doing in the moment you are doing it. Notice if your thoughts are drifting to the past or future. Notice if you are meditating on feelings of regret, anger, or worry based on past circumstances or situations. On purpose bring your attention back to what you are doing at the present moment and focus on that. You might have to get a scripture to focus on to help. If you are having serious issues focusing on the present, it might be time to enlist the help of a professional counselor to assist you in this area.

CHAPTER 4

THE NATURE AND CHARACTER OF GOD

HEALING IS ONE OF the most confusing areas of the Christian experience for some. However, it really is the simplest of Christian truths to accept. I already know what you are thinking… "how can this be so? I have been contending with my sickness and disease for years!" This truth becomes simple to those who have a genuine Biblically-based knowledge and understanding of the nature or character of God. Most Christians do not know God well enough to realize His heart towards His people. We gain knowledge and understanding of God first and foremost through His Word, the Bible. The Bible says that God is a God of love (1 John 4:16). God demonstrated His love for us by the sacrifice of His only begotten son Jesus (John 3:16). This asks you to ponder the question, "How can a loving God desire that His children suffer?" It is not the heart of God that we suffer in this life with sickness and disease. God sent His son Jesus to be the final sacrifice for sin and sickness. By accepting sickness and disease as the will of God, you are in turn saying that God's sacrifice of Jesus was not good enough!

The thief cometh not, but for to steal, and to kill, and to destroy: I am come that they might have life, and that they

40

might have it more abundantly.

-- John 10: 10

John 10:10 is a good description of the nature of God versus the nature of the enemy. The nature of the devil is to steal, kill, and destroy. So here is your test: anything you are facing that steals from you, attempts to kill you or destroy you is not from God! God's nature is to give. He came to give us life! Some might be saying, "What about the judgement of God. I do not deserve to be healed. This is God's punishment for my terrible behavior!" My answer to you is that yes, we serve a God who judges sin. We can see this throughout the Old Testament. However, with acceptance of Jesus Christ you have been made righteous, a son or daughter of God (2 Corinthians 5:21). This comes with certain rights and privileges. Christ became sin for us and suffered the penalty of sin for us, so we do not have to suffer! Unlike those in the Old Testament, Jesus has become our advocate and goes to the Father on our behalf and grace is extended.

If death and dying are the will of God, why don't you do more to be in the will of God? Why do you go to the doctor and take measures to not be in the will of God? You see as we go further along this line of logic, it gets more and more ridiculous. However, this is the lie that a lot of Christians choose to believe forsaking the clear truths in the Word of God. Please do not be deceived any longer! Study the truths of the word of God yourself in this area and let the Holy Spirit show you God's true will for you – life and health. We must understand that it is in the character of God to want you healed, whole, and well. He gave the ultimate gift for this to be a reality in your life.

Surely he hath borne our griefs, and carried our sorrows: yet we did esteem him stricken, smitten of God, and afflicted. But he was wounded for our transgressions, he was bruised for our iniquities: the chastisement of our peace was upon him; and with his stripes we are healed.

-- Isaiah 53: 4-5

God provided the solution to the sin problem and everything that came with it in the person of Jesus Christ. We just have to accept Him and what He did for us.

The character God is the character of faith. The character of faith is victory. We must get on the victory-side of things concerning the promises of God, especially regarding our health and healing. The opposite side of victory is defeat. Defeat is a mental stronghold which must be destroyed by the Word of God. So often, we can let situations and circumstances attempt to control and manipulate us into believing the opposite of faith and the opposite of God's will. We must understand three essential keys to get on the victory-side in our life.

1. You must have an expectation of victory.
2. You must have a revelation of God's goodness.
3. You must praise and worship God despite what you see in the natural.

Let's examine each key and how it can help us walk on the victory-side concerning our health and healing.

You Must Have an Expectation of Victory

We must expect victorious outcomes in our lives. Expectation is a characteristic of faith. The Bible says that our expectation is from God (Psalms 62:5) and it will not be cut off (Proverbs 23:18). The Bible uses the same Hebrew word for expectation as hope. In the New Testament, hope can also be interchanged with expectation and trust.

Now faith is the substance of things hoped for, the evidence of things not seen.

-- Hebrews 11:1

You cannot have faith without hope or expectation. Expectation is one of the building blocks of faith. We build our expectation in God by having a firm knowledge and understanding of who He is and what He is capable of doing. This understanding comes primarily through God's Word. We can read about all the times that God saw others through to victory. We can see the insurmountable circumstances that these individuals were faced with and yet they still overcame. The common factor was their belief, trust, and reliance in God. This type of trust can be developed. We must commit to developing a more intimate relationship with Him.

You Must Have a Revelation of God's Goodness

We serve a good God! We serve a God that wants us healed. It is the enemy that comes to steal, kill, and destroy (John 10:10). This is something we must understand to be able to receive the promises of God. God wants to bless us! He wants to see us healed, set free, and delivered more than we want it for ourselves. We need to upgrade our mindset to this type of thinking. If you truly do not believe that God is a good God, but rather is a hard judge for instance, it will affect how you receive from God. It will affect your faith. Why? Because it will affect your expectation. We just saw the connection between faith and expectation. Your expectation is so important when receiving from God.

You Must Praise and Worship God Despite What We See in the Natural

At times it can be challenging to stay in faith when what you see in the natural is the opposite of what we are believing for God to do. When symptoms of sickness and disease persist despite our prayers, it can be discouraging. This is normal. Sometimes we do not want to admit that this part of believing God is challenging. This is also one of the main reasons it is so hard for people to see the end of their faith.

Let us hold tightly without wavering to the hope we affirm,
for God can be trusted to keep his promise.

-- Hebrews 10:23 NLT

Praise and worship to God can assist in keeping your mind focused on Him and His promises despite what you see in the natural. It is also a corresponding action of your faith. Reminding yourself of the promises of God and reading about His faithfulness to others in the Word of God will strengthen your faith. It will keep you motivated and inspired.

Faith Failures

When we do not see the promises of God realized in our life, it can cause us to believe an assortment of things, especially in the area of healing. This is often where we see some of the "experience-based" teaching and doctrine that comes out of Christian circles. Theories like, "God uses sickness to teach you something", "It is God's will for you to be sick," and the list goes on. These are often an individual's way of coping and rationalizing why they did not receive certain promises from God. They believe God has failed them. It causes them to believe that their faith in God does not work. Some people believe the lie of the enemy and use these experiences to push them away from God. The truth of the matter is we do not know everything in our natural minds. However, the spirit of God knows all things.

But it was to us that God revealed these things by his Spirit.
For his Spirit searches out everything and shows us God's
deep secrets.

-- 1 Corinthians 2:10 NLT

We must ask Him "the why" behind the reality of certain outcomes that we have in our life. This takes time spent with God and prayer in the spirit. The Bible speaks of prayer in the spirit as a way to pray out divine mysteries. Prayer in the spirit is a gift given to the body of Christ.

> *For he who speaks in a tongue does not speak to men but to God, for no one understands him; however, in the spirit he speaks mysteries.*
>
> -- 1 Corinthians 14:2 NKJV

You can find out more about praying in the spirit via speaking in other tongues by clicking this link to get to the bonus material for this book here http://bit.ly/gshbookbonus (password: healing). Sometimes we do not know exactly why certain things happen. Praying in other tongues can help.

There is a Connection Between Strongholds and Trauma

Faith failures are often rooted in negative past experience and traumas. If we have a loved one that we prayed for to be healed, and they died, or we had a traumatic experience like persistent abuse, which caused us to feel abandoned by God are just a couple of the issues of life which can affect our faith and our relationship with God. At this point, we must go back to our foundation, God loves us. He is the author of life and wants to see us completely healed and whole. We have a real enemy, Satan, who hates God. We also live in a sin-filled world. We have to be prepared for the attacks of the enemy, and the things that can come by just living in this world.

Everything that happens to us is not necessary a result of a direct attack from the enemy. Some issues that we deal with are a result of our bad decisions and lack of operating in wisdom. Thank God, He is there to help us regardless of the origin of our problems. The key is acknowledging Him in all our ways, so he can bring success our way (Joshua 1:8-9). The Bible says, we can ask God for wisdom and He will give it to us liberally (James 1:5)! Halleluiah! As a nationally certified health educator, it would be shameful to not mention good stewardship of the body that God gave us. We have to take care of this temple through healthy nutrition, rest, physical activity, and behaviors which cause us to get the best use out of our bodies. This is wisdom. The knowledge is there for us to live a healthy life. God has made healing available for us. However, we must practice discipline regarding eating right and exercising, so that we are not actively destroying God's temple. This is good stewardship. Common, preventable diseases should not be named among us which result from poor discipline and stewardship of our bodies. If this describes you, decide today to commit to live a healthier life with God's help.

Past traumas and stresses not only affect us naturally which leads to less than optimal mental and physical health, but also affect our spiritual health. Past traumas are the foundation of negative strongholds. As we discussed in the last chapter, strongholds are a firmly fortified set of values or beliefs that have been established in the mind and/or emotions often triggered by a circumstances, experiences, or events. The simple definition of trauma is an experience(s) which causes significant distress or disturbance to an individual. In a majority of cases, this experience is associated with a person, place, or thing which holds significance and authority in an individual's life. In Chapter 3, we discussed trauma in more detail. In this Chapter, we will address traumas that we experience as they relate to strongholds in our life. Often faith failures are connected to the strongholds that have been built in our thought lives.

The Building Blocks of Strongholds

In my study I have found strongholds to be built from six distinct items. These items are

1. Word curses (negative words spoken over you or to you).

2. Traumatic Pictures

3. Inner Vows

4. Negative Expectations and Beliefs

5. Soul Ties

6. Generational Iniquity (patterns of sin on generational line aka generational curses)

In the chart below, I have provided definitions to all of these terms.

Stronghold Building Block	Definition
Word Curses	Negative words spoken over you or to you usually from someone whom you have or have had a close relationship with.
Traumatic Pictures	A memory/vision of an event or experience which caused great pain or stress in your heart (brokenheartedness).
Inner Vows	The conscious or unconscious promises or statements an individual makes as a result of negative expectations/beliefs. Also, described as self-cursing.
Negative Expectation and Beliefs	Negative belief systems which are contrary to the Word of God. These belief systems are powered by the enemy. These belief systems are often associated with painful or traumatic experiences.
Soul Ties	A covenant or attachment with another person or with God often demonstrated by a close committed relationship by which a person's mind, will, and emotions are attached to another person, place, or thing.
Generational Curses and Iniquity	Patterns of sin in your generational line

These six building blocks individually or collectively contribute to the strongholds that we have in our lives. It is our duty to recognize which of these items are causing certain thought patterns and belief systems in our lives. At times, we are unaware to our acceptance and agreement with stronghold building blocks. It takes discernment. This will take time with the Holy Spirit, prayer, and meditation in the Word of God. Any strongholds which have rooted themselves in your life can be destroyed. It will take a partnership with the Holy Spirit, but it can be done. Coming into alignment and agreement with the enemy concerning any of the above will make you and those you are ministering to a target for demonic activity, sickness, and disease.

What are You in Agreement with?

To better understand how agreement with the thoughts attached to these strongholds function, let's define the term agreement. Agreement is defined as 1. Concord; harmony; conformity. 2. Union of opinions or sentiments; 3. Resemblance; conformity; similitude. 4. Union of minds in regard to a transfer of interest; bargain; compact; contract; stipulation[1]. From this definition, we can see that agreeing with something involves your intellect, thoughts, and opinions. Each of the stronghold building blocks has a series of thoughts and emotions attached to it based on your negative experiences. For example, you could have possibly had an emotionally distant or absentee father in your home. The enemy can attack you in one or more of the building blocks of these strongholds.

For example, due to your father being emotionally distant, he could say things to you repeatedly which tear down your self-worth or self-esteem. Or because of the way he treats you, you speak negative words (word curses) over yourself and you make promises to yourself like, "I will never be like my dad" or "I hate myself and don't deserve to live" (inner vows). You believe you are not intelligent and will not be successful in life because of what your father said (negative expectations/beliefs). After all, no one in your family has been successful and always end up falling into the same bad circumstances (generational iniquity). But you cannot get your father's words and actions out of your mind. You always refer to them when you are faced with certain situations and fear overcomes your heart (soul tie).

As we can see by this example, the effects of negative strongholds are far-reaching and can affect every area of our life. Taking our example, you can see how someone dealing with this level of stress and trauma could be susceptible to attack from the enemy with things like depression, suicide, chronic pain, among other things. I would recommend someone like this to first, forgive their father. Then renounce or reject the agreements that they have made with the word curses, inner vows, negative experiences, and generational iniquity. I would encourage them to discover who they truly are in Christ, and that they are loved by Him. I would encourage this person to seek prayer for freedom at their local church or with a ministry that they trust. In this situation, follow-up counseling would also be needed to replace all of the negative thinking patterns with godly thinking, actions, and habits. The accountability and support of counseling would help this individual tremendously. If this example is similar to your own life, commit today to seek the proper resources to see deliverance and lasting healing in your life today!

If we are allowing faith failures to affect our lives and nurture negative strongholds, our faith is not rooted and grounded in the Word of God, but in ours or someone else's experience. This feeds doubt and unbelief in our lives. This could be one of the reasons that you find it so hard to believe God or see the end or good results of your faith. These are all questions for the Holy Spirit. You might be saying the right things but believing opposite of what you are saying. You agree with the negative strongholds and past experiences more than the Word of God.

So Jesus answered and said to them, "Have faith in God. For assuredly, I say to you, whoever says to this mountain, 'Be removed and be cast into the sea,' and does not doubt in his heart, but believes that those things he says will be done, he will have whatever he says. Therefore I say to you, whatever things you ask when you pray, believe that you receive them, and you will have them.

-- Mark 11:22-24 NKJV

Our agreement will determine our results. Examine what you have come into agreement with and commit to uproot those agreements which are outside of the will of God.

The Problem of Sin-Consciousness

Sin is missing the mark. The mark includes God's way of doing things found in the Bible. Often, we are in agreement with the old sinful man of the flesh, and we do not have understanding of our new life or union in Christ.

Therefore if any person is [ingrafted] in Christ (the Messiah) he is a new creation (a new creature altogether); the old [previous moral and spiritual condition] has passed away. Behold, the fresh and new has come! But all things are from God, Who through Jesus Christ reconciled us to Himself [received us into favor, brought us into harmony with Himself] and gave to us the ministry of reconciliation [that by word and deed we might aim to bring others into harmony with Him]. It was God [personally present] in Christ, reconciling and restoring the world to favor with Himself, not counting up and holding against [men] their trespasses [but cancelling them], and committing to us the message of reconciliation (of the restoration to favor). So we are Christ's ambassadors, God making His appeal as it were through us. We [as Christ's personal representatives] beg you for His sake to lay hold of the divine favor [now offered to you] and be reconciled to God. For our sake He made Christ [virtually] to be sin Who knew no sin, so that in and through Him we might become [endued with, viewed as being in, and examples of] the righteousness of God [what we ought to be, approved and acceptable and in right relationship with Him, by His goodness].

-- 2 Corinthians 5:17-21 AMPC

We have been made into new creatures with the death, burial, and resurrection of Jesus Christ. The character of faith is grounded in our acceptance and agreement with this reality. The reality that we have been declared righteous with this single act. God has declared and made us righteous through no act of our own. We were declared righteous (justified) based on what was done in Calvary over 2000 years ago. When we see the words "justified" in the Bible, it is the same as saying declared righteous or approved by God.

Having been declared righteous, then, by faith, we have peace toward God through our Lord Jesus Christ, through whom also we have the access by the faith into this grace in which we have stood, and we boast on the hope of the glory of God.

-- Romans 5:1-2 YLT

Righteousness is defined as "the ability to stand in the presence of the Father God without the sense of guilt or inferiority."[2] God wants us to live with a consciousness of our righteousness. He wants our thinking to agree with this reality. However, our old sin nature is more comfortable focusing and agreeing with having a sin consciousness. Sin Consciousness is defined as the inferiority complex of man as a result of the Fall. It is man's sense of fear, guilt, condemnation, inferiority, failure, and weakness which leads us to not follow Christ's ways. We must renew our mind (Romans 12:1-2) to our new nature and all that goes with it to have a different reality that drives our actions and thinking. Those operating out of sin consciousness allow sin, death and Satan to rule their lives. A sin consciousness operates in an unbeliever who has not accepted Christ and in believers who do not have a revelation of whom they are in Christ. A sin consciousness is destroyed though the impartation and realization of the divine nature of Christ given at the point of salvation. The old sin nature must be put down and a new divine nature must be put on.

Christ is for you! It is His character to bless you. However, mind-sets outside of the Word of God contribute to short-circuiting the power of God from fully working in our lives. God's character is the character of love. He is fully devoted to you. Are you fully devoted to Him?

Do you have the Correct Picture of God?

What is your picture of God? Oftentimes we have the "churchy" or religious answer to this question. We will say what people want to hear. We will say that God loves us. He is a loving Father. This is true, but do you really believe that? Do your actions agree with the statements which you profess? We need to examine our lives and actions to determine where you stand on this issue. Do you truly see God as a loving father? Or do you see God as a judge, waiting to punish you when you do something outside of His will or plan? Or do you see God as a lofty King which gives you orders, and it is slavery being a child of Him?

Only time spent with the Father and listening to the Holy Spirit will help you identify where you are on this continuum. If you do not see God as a loving Father, you are most likely operating out of a heart of an orphan rather than the heart of a son. This is also called having an orphan heart. An orphan heart is bread in religious environments. Environments staunch in rules, regulations, without the true love of Jesus which is bathed in freedom. Having an orphan heart causes a person to be insecure because he does not know if his or her service to God is enough. This individual is working for God's approval. This person needs acceptance, affirmation, and praise from people. This person serves God out of duty and not pleasure. This person feels guilt and shame when he or she feels like they do not live up to God's expectations. This person has a sin consciousness.

A person with an orphan heart does not have a close and intimate relationship with God. His or her relationship is often cold and distant. It is a slave/servant and master type of relationship. This and other erroneous views of God often originate with the relationship we had with our Father. These father wounds cause us to have a skewed view of the Heavenly Father based on the mistreatment we receive from our natural father or father figure. The cure for this is time spent in the presence of God and in the Word of God. We must abide in God (John 15:1-7).

> *Abide in me, and I in you. As the branch cannot bear fruit of itself, except it abide in the vine; no more can ye, except ye abide in me. I am the vine, ye are the branches: He that abideth in me, and I in him, the same bringeth forth much fruit: for without me ye can do nothing. If ye abide in me, and my words abide in you, ye shall ask what ye will, and it shall be done unto you. Herein is my Father glorified, that ye bear much fruit; so shall ye be my disciples.*

> -- John 15: 4-5, 7-8

Abide means to dwell with on a continuous basis. To abide, we must continuously acknowledge God in our lives. This means that you walk throughout your day recognizing that God with you. You speak to Him throughout your day and dialogue with Him. This is truly abiding. In doing this, you will experience God continually. The Holy Spirit will speak to your heart and shave off those rough edges that are not like God in your character. You will begin to see with the eyes of Christ. In that seeing, the Holy Spirit will give you the correct picture of God, a picture of love. The key is our surrender. We must surrender to the process of becoming more like Christ, to developing His mind, and His way of doing things. This comes through abiding in His presence continually, praying in the Spirit, and renewing our mind with the Word of God.

God's Character Can Be Seen Through His Word

God's character is demonstrated through the Word of God. One of my favorite passages in the Bible is John chapter 1.

> *In the beginning was the Word, and the Word was with God, and the Word was God. The same was in the beginning with God. All things were made by him; and without him was not anything made that was made. In him was life; and the life was the light of men. And the light shineth in darkness; and the darkness comprehended it not. But as many as received him, to them gave he power to become the sons of God, even to them that believe on his name.*
>
> -- John 1:1-5, 12

The Word has always been with us since the beginning. The Word was made flesh in the person of Jesus Christ. Jesus was the perfect illustration of the Word of God. We can examine His life as a guide to living by the Word of God. However, you will only learn how to move and think as He did by meditating in the Word of God. Through meditation, we renew our minds and get God's perspective on things. The Word teaches us to think like He does. We gain the mind of Christ (1 Corinthians 2:16). Check out the bonus items for this book for more resources on mediation on the Word of God.

Knowing God's Word helps you to know His character. His character is the character of faith. Knowing God's Word increases our discernment and helps with our ability to hear His voice. If you have problems believing God for something, get into His Word. An individual's lack of Word level is directly correlated to their ability to believe God's promises. You must have your own revelation of the Word of God for it to be active and operative in your life. Having a "head" knowledge of the Word is not enough. You must have an intimate relationship with the author of the Word to bring it into life. You must not just know about God, but you must know God by His Spirit.

> *For as many as are led by the Spirit of God, they are the sons of God.*
>
> -- Romans 8:14

The parable of the sower speaks of various things that can hinder how you receive the Word (Mark 4:1-20).

> *The sower soweth the word. And these are they by the way side, where the word is sown; but when they have heard, Satan cometh immediately, and taketh away the word that was sown in their hearts. And these are they likewise which are sown on stony ground; who, when they have heard the word, immediately receive it with gladness; And have no root in themselves, and so endure but for a time: afterward, when affliction or persecution ariseth for the word's sake, immediately they are offended. And these are they which are sown among thorns; such as hear the word, And the cares of this world, and the deceitfulness of riches, and the lusts of other things entering in, choke the word, and it becometh unfruitful. And these are they which are sown on good ground; such as hear the word, and receive it, and bring forth fruit, some thirtyfold, some sixty, and some a hundred.*
>
> -- Mark 4:14-20

The ground is the ground of our heart. What kind of ground are you? When you read the Word and meditate on the promises what happens? When you read the Word do other thoughts and reasonings come to your mind opposite of the Word; thoughts that cause you to doubt the Word? Do these thoughts cause you to believe that the promise is not true for you? If so, this is the seed that has fallen by the wayside and it will not produce the desired harvest.

Do you receive the Word when you initially hear it or read it and you are excited about it? You keep that excitement for a period of time. Then when circumstances or symptoms in the case of healing come, do you begin to believe in the circumstances or symptoms more than the Word? For instance, when people think bad of you for believing the promise of God, you get discouraged and believe the people's word over God's Word. If this happens, the Word was sewn on stony ground; you will not receive your intended harvest. Affliction and persecution stole the Word from your heart and the intended harvest is not produced.

Do you hear the Word and receive it, but you forget what the Word said or rather do not hold the Word as priority in your life? Do you let the busyness of life and other things cause the Word of God to be second, third, fourth, or fifth priority? Or do things or avenues of the world seem easier than believing the Word of God? If this is the case, the Word was sewn among thorns. The Word will be unfruitful, and you will not receive the expected harvest.

The last and best type of soil or ground is when you hear the Word and receive it. You do not let anything steal the Word and revelation of that Word you received. You do not allow thoughts and reasonings opposite of the Word come in and get you off your stance. You do not let persecution or affliction come in and you do not get distracted with the cares of the world. You hold the Word above all and first priority. You are not moved when the situation and circumstance look to be opposite of what you are believing. The Word was sewn on good ground and it will always produce a great result and harvest. We endeavor for our hearts to always be good ground in every area of our lives. However, we must give ourselves to the truths of the Word and meditate on them to have the results we desire.

Wholeness and Peace Come Through Abiding

Wholeness and peace are the results of abiding in God. Wholeness means you have nothing missing and nothing broken in your life. You have all you need. Peace and wholeness go hand in hand. Christ came and died for our salvation. Within the salvation package is peace and wholeness. The Word "save" in the Bible is translated as sozo in the Greek.

Sozo (Grk.) = heal, preserve, save (self), do well, be (make) whole, to save, to keep safe and sound, to rescue from danger or destruction, from injury or peril, to save a suffering one (from perishing), that is one suffering from disease, to make well, to heal, restore to health, to preserve one from danger of destruction, to rescue.[3]

We can see the richness of this word in this definition. When you accept Jesus Christ as your personal Lord and Savior, you have access to the promises of God which include all that the word sozo has to offer. You just have to appropriate or access the promises by faith, believe that you receive and act like it. Then you will have those things you desire. Abiding in the presence of God leads to developing His mind and becoming more like Him.

Sozo is God's gift to the believer. We are meant to live the abundant life. Abiding in Christ causes us to continually partake or receive sozo in our lives. Our peace and understanding of the operation of sozo in our lives is a byproduct of meditation in the Word, prayer, and fellowship with God. This also relates to knowing God as Father and understanding His character and ways. God is waiting on us. He wants to develop a close intimate relationship with us. This goes beyond experiencing God just as a way to get something out of Him. This cannot be our main purpose in desiring to cultivate a relationship with Him. You must understand relationship goes way beyond just receiving the promises of God. Our focus in knowing God must be simply rooted in understanding our Father, who He is and what makes Him uniquely Him. This is the definition of pure love, intimacy, and worship. We love God for who He is with no conditions and not based on what He has or has not done for us. We grow to know Him deeply and in turn love Him and His character.

Activation Prayer

Father, I pray that you keep me in the center of your will. I pray I grow to know you deeply and experience your over whelming love for me. Lord, show me myself. Show me where I have been deficient in my love for you. I thank you God that I know you and I understand your character. I live by your faith and pursue your purposes for my life. I abide in you and live in your peace, your sozo. This peace permeates every aspect and component of my existence. Thank you for these things and more. Amen.

Next Steps

1. Examine how you view God. Ask yourself if you truly know and understand His character. In your journal write down your thoughts on these topics. Pray and ask God to show you yourself in this area. Are you just seeking God for His hand (what He can do for you) or His heart (knowing Him)?

2. Ask yourself if you are letting past experiences, traumas, or strongholds skew your picture of God. Ask God to show you these areas in your life. Write down in your journal the words, thoughts, and impressions you receive. Ask the Lord where do you start in changing your current pictures and reversing the negative effects of these traumas, experiences, and strongholds.

Make notes on these things in your journal.

3. Read and meditate on John 14:15-17 and John 15:1-16. In your journal write down what these passages mean to you in your life. Pray and ask God to reveal to you how these scriptures should guide you in your everyday life. Write down in your journal the words, thoughts, and impressions you receive.

Prescription for Divine Health: Practicing Solitude

Make practicing solitude a priority in your life. Take some time daily to quiet yourself. Go to a quiet environment with minimal to no distractions. Do not think on anything but Jesus. Are you able to do it? If not, take baby steps. Start with five minutes and work your way up. This will help your mind to rest and bring about better health. You will also find yourself having more focused times of prayer. This is especially needed to maintain good mental and emotional health.

CHAPTER 5

QUESTIONS ABOUT HEALING

Why so many questions?

When it comes to healing, many schools of thought, opinion, and philosophy exist. Often these things are rooted in an individual's interpretation of the Bible, doctrinal background, or past experience. Often there is a mixture of all three of these aspects. As we have stated throughout this text, God is a good God that wants us well. We have an enemy, Satan, that does everything within his power to stop God's plan from occurring in our lives. He is the author of sickness and disease.

Regardless, of what is happening around us and the pain or suffering that we might feel, we must stay focused on the promises of God. The author of healing was sent to die, so that we can live in divine health all the days of our life.

> *Who Himself bore our sins in His own body on the tree, that we, having died to sins, might live for righteousness—by whose stripes you were healed.*
>
> -- 1 Peter 2:24 NKJV

The Word of God is our final authority, regardless of what we see with our eyes. If this is not a reality to you in your life and doubt and unbelief fill your heart regarding God Word, take the time to analyze why this is the case. Ask the Lord for help in renewing your mind.

Dealing with Your Negative Past Experiences

Often negative past experiences create seeds of doubt and unbelief in our heart. We water these seeds with further negative images and words which agree with the thoughts that are not aligned with the promises of God.

> *Casting down imaginations, and every high thing that exalteth itself against the knowledge of God, and bringing into captivity every thought to the obedience of Christ;*

> -- 2 Corinthians 10:5

As this scripture states these thoughts, words, and images must be cast down and replaced with the Word of God. This means that there is something that we must do. We must study and meditate the Word of God pertaining to His healing promises. There are some scriptures in this books bonus material to get you started (http://bit.ly/gshbookbonus).

Depending on the past trauma that you might have experienced, believing God for someone to be healed or experiencing God not moving in the area of healing in your life, may have affected you in a way which makes it tremendously hard to believe God in these areas. Often these thoughts and images create fear in your heart which causes you to reject faith. In this rejection of faith, we can begin to question God, His motives, and His Word. This can cause us to rationalize and interpret the Word based on our past negative experience. This often creates cognitive dissonance in our souls.

Cognitive dissonance is defined as "mental discomfort (psychological stress) experienced by a person who simultaneously holds two or more contradictory beliefs, ideas, or values. The occurrence of cognitive dissonance is a consequence of a person's performing an action that contradicts personal beliefs, ideals, and values; and also, occurs when confronted with new information that contradicts said beliefs, ideals, and values."[1] Cognitive dissonance is the result of some of us attempting to believe God's Word, but also intimately believing past traumas or experiences which impact our hearts intentions and actions. This creates a disagreement in our souls. What you are in agreement with will determine and impact the results that you receive when believing.

How do we correct this cognitive dissonance in our souls? The answer is one word, consistency. We must uproot the strongholds or negative belief systems in our hearts. We must be real with ourselves about what truly exists in our hearts. It is impacting our well-being and our ability to receive results. These negative strongholds and belief systems are uprooted by the Word of God and prayer. At times these strongholds can become empowered by the demonic. If this is the case, seeking out a mature believer or minister will be necessary to walk you through gaining freedom. Study and meditation in the Word of God is also an essential component of this process.

> *For the word of God is quick, and powerful, and sharper than any two-edged sword, piercing even to the dividing asunder of soul and spirit, and of the joints and marrow, and is a discerner of the thoughts and intents of the heart.*
>
> -- Hebrews 4:12

In this reference, the Word of God can be seen as a "filter" to our souls (mind, will, & emotions). You only allow the Word to be a filter to the degree of your knowledge, understanding, and revelation of it. Filters are designed to hold back, separate elements, or modify the appearance of something. The Word of God or Bible is our filter in this life. We use it to make judgements and it enables us to operate from a Biblical world-view. The message of the Word is summed up in the message of love. Once we uproot these negative strongholds or belief systems, we must replace them with the Word of God. Some of us, must put accountability measures in place to help. This can be in the form of engaging in small group ministry, Biblical counseling, Biblical mentorship or discipleship. These are all great methods of helping us to live out a victorious Christian life and experience.

Exposing the Spirit of Error

At times, questions come to us regarding God's reason and methods of healing as the result of coming into agreement with a spirit of error.

> *We are from God; he who knows God listens to us; he who is not from God does not listen to us. By this we know the spirit of truth and the spirit of error.*
>
> -- 1 John 4:6 NAS

You have to discern when a spirit of error exists. In my experience, I have just had a knowing that something did not feel right. For me it has just been a slight "nudge" or "check" in my spirit. This nudge causes me to investigate the scriptures and more concerning the person delivering the message. Through this investigation, I often find something is off with the message or the person delivering the message has issues and his or her fruit does not align with what is being taught. What might this look like? The minister might have long-lasting character issues, or his/her other material also has hints of non-Biblical based teaching. This can be teaching rooted in the New Age movement, mysticism, among other things. The person might also be one who manipulates to gain wealth. We just need to be sensitive to the Holy Spirit and follow the peace of God. However, if you do not know the Word of God, it will be hard for you to discern or distinguish what is truth and what is error.

> *Beware of false prophets, who come to you in sheep's clothing, but inwardly they are ravenous wolves. You will know them by their fruits. Do men gather grapes from thorn bushes or figs from thistles? Even so, every good tree bears good fruit, but a bad tree bears bad fruit. A good tree cannot bear bad fruit, nor can a bad tree bear good fruit. Every tree that does not bear good fruit is cut down and thrown into the fire. Therefore, by their fruits you will know them.*

-- Mathew 7:15-20 NKJV

God gave gifts to aid us in avoiding the spirit of error in the world. These gifts come in those called to the five-fold ministry. It is the apostles, prophets, evangelists, pastors, and teachers that are commissioned to teach and lead the Body of Christ in the way of truth.

> *And it is he who gifted some to be apostles, others to be prophets, others to be evangelists, and still others to be pastors and teachers, to equip the saints, to do the work of ministry, and to build up the body of the Messiah until all of us are united in the faith and in the full knowledge of God's Son, and until we attain mature adulthood and the full standard of development in the Messiah. Then we will no longer be little children, tossed like waves and blown about by every wind of doctrine, by people's trickery, or by clever strategies that would lead us astray. Instead, by speaking the truth in love, we will grow up completely and become one with the head, that is, one with the Messiah...*

-- Ephesians 4:11-15 ISV

Unfortunately, there are some who proclaim to be five-fold ministry gifts who operate from a spirit of error. Therefore, we have to let our spirits and the Word of God be our guide.

Exposing the Religious Spirit

Lastly, we must examine our beliefs and determine if we are operating or in agreement with a spirit of religion. The term religion here is defined as ritual and other man-made works by which someone is attempting to access God or the things of God. In this sense, religion is the opposite of relationship. A true relationship with God goes beyond Christian ritualistic behavior. The difference between religion and relationship is grounded in the intentions of your heart. Is your spiritual service based in your desire to work hard enough to make God appreciate you, thereby earning God's acceptance, approval, or appreciation? Or make others think you are spiritual? If this is the case, you might be coming into agreement with a spirit of religion.

A religious spirit is one of the hallmarks of the last days. We are in the last days and are awaiting the return of Christ.

> *They will hold to an outward form of godliness but deny its power. Stay away from such people.*
> -- 2 Timothy 3:5 ISV

These individuals have a form of Christianity but is not the real thing. At times, we unknowingly come into agreement with spirits of religion. This is often based in our own feelings of insufficiency and unrighteousness. We become more conscious of our sin-nature rather than our God-nature. This type of thinking will naturally cause us to try to earn God's approval as justification of His love for us.

Due to this persistent struggle to be pleasing to God, it causes questions to arise in our heart as to why God has not healed me yet. These questions are based in our religious belief systems. A person like this believes that they have not done enough to "earn" their healing. They have not read the word enough; they have not confessed enough scriptures.... You see where I am going with this. However, this type of thinking is grounded in unbelief and "works" righteousness. Healing is a free gift given to believers and unbelievers. We must trust God that at the moment we pray, despite what it looks like in the natural that we are healed, because God's Word says it.

Common Questions About Healing

In my experience, there are a number of questions which most people seeking healing tend to ask themselves. In the next few pages I have listed some of the most common questions that I have seen asked about receiving healing. You may have asked some of these questions yourself.

Is Healing for All?

Healing is encompassed in the Salvation package. It is just as much God's will for all to be saved as it is for all to be healed (1 Timothy 2:4). For you to complete the purposes of God in the Earth, it is God's best, for you to have a healed and whole body. If it were not God's will to heal all this line of logic would cause us to be in error and opposite of the will of God if we prayed or contended for sickness and disease to be removed from a person's body.

In terms of salvation, there are no barriers. Anyone can become saved and have a relationship with Jesus. According to John 3:16, God wishes all to be saved and come into the knowledge of the truth. The only seeming barriers to salvation are the man-made ones based in religion. Romans 10:8-10 provide the instructions to receiving God's salvation.

> *But what does it say? "The word is near you, in your mouth and in your heart" (that is, the word of faith which we preach): that if you confess with your mouth the Lord Jesus and believe in your heart that God has raised Him from*

the dead, you will be saved. For with the heart one believes unto righteousness, and with the mouth confession is made unto salvation.

-- Romans 10:8-10 NKJV

If healing is in the salvation package and salvation is available to all, then healing is available to all. In the last chapter, we discussed the peace of God and wholeness. During this discussion, we examined the Greek meaning of the word 'saved' which is sozo. The word sozo is used 110 times in the Bible. As a review, the definition is:

Sozo (Grk.) = heal, preserve, save (self), do well, be (make) whole, to save, to keep safe and sound, to rescue from danger or destruction, from injury or peril, to save a suffering one (from perishing), that is one suffering from disease, to make well, to heal, restore to health, to preserve one from danger of destruction, to rescue[2].

Your healing was purchased at the time of your salvation.

At times the follow-up thought to this question comes regarding people who die believing. In our life, we can come across people who were believing God for healing and still die. This is used to uphold the belief that it is not God's will for all to be healed. If this is your belief, you are holding your experience above the Word of God. Truthfully, I do not know why some people die believing. The Bible says that "the secret things belong to the Lord" in Deuteronomy 29:29. We will not know everything until we get to be in glory with God. However, if this is the case, they are in good company with Sarah and Abraham who also died believing.

By faith Sarah herself also received strength to conceive seed, and she bore a child when she was past the age, because she judged Him faithful who had promised. Therefore from one man, and him as good as dead, were born as many as the stars of the sky in multitude—innumerable as the sand which is by the seashore. These all died in faith, not having received the promises, but having seen them afar off were assured of them, embraced them and confessed that they were strangers and pilgrims on the earth.

-- Hebrews 11:11-13 NKJV

This verse says that Sarah, Abraham and others died in faith. They never saw the multitude after them that would be part of their lineage; but they continued believing.

Is my sickness for the glory of God?

If this statement were true, why do you pray for sickness to go away? Shouldn't you be praying for the worst sickness there is to come on you to receive more of God's glory? Also, Jesus our example walked in the fullness of the anointing, and He NEVER walked in sickness and disease. He always was giving God glory by the good works he did. He did not make people sick to glorify God. If this were true hospitals would be considered places of God's greatest glory, since it is full of sickness and disease. The further we walk down this path of reasoning, the more ridiculous it seems. Sickness and disease are not now or will ever be a demonstration of God's glory!

The story of Lazarus is another reason people might believe in this way.

When Jesus heard that, He said, "This sickness is not unto death, but for the glory of God, that the Son of God may be glorified through it.

-- John 11:4 NKJV

In this verse, it seems as if God receives glory in our sickness and death. Well-meaning people have taken this verse to fit their experience. However, they do not finish reading. If you finish the story in context, you will see that Jesus actually heals Lazarus and raises him from the dead. In this miracle, God was glorified. When someone is raised from the dead, it takes at minimum three gifts of the spirit in manifestation. The gift of faith is needed, so you can believe that the individual can live. This gift is needed so that you even step out. Then the working of miracles actually raises the person from the dead and the gifts of healing is needed so the person doesn't die again from what killed them in the first place! When this is happening, I do not believe you analyze what exactly is going on at the time, but potentially, these are the most likely gifts to be in operation.

The reality of the situation is that Lazarus did die, but Jesus was speaking prophetically at this moment, possibly operating in a word of knowledge or wisdom, stating what was to happen in this situation. The end of the story is that Jesus raised him from the dead (John 11:43-44). As a result of this miracle, many of the Jews believed in Jesus (v. 45). In this God was glorified.

Has God allowed sickness in my body to teach me something?

This is also a question that has arisen out of individuals' disappointment and experience. It is demonic in its origin. The Bible says that God gives good gifts to his children (Matthew 7:11). God does not need to use a tool of the enemy – sickness and disease (John 10:10) to teach you something. This erroneous belief is further upheld by those who as a result of their sickness and disease do something great for others or society. Yes, God wants you to walk in greatness in your life; however, he does not need sickness and disease to do it. Sickness and disease can be seen as a motivator. It can motivate you to do everything in your power to get out of your situation, or you can do nothing. I thank God for those who have exercised their will while fighting disease to help others in the same fight. I believe God strengthens these people in their affliction. God is able to turn any situation around for His good. He can and will inevitably get the glory on the Earth and in Heaven.

The Word also says that faith comes or arises by hearing the Word of God (Romans 10:17). Nowhere does it say that sickness and disease increase your faith. As a result of contending for your healing, you might increase your Bible study and renewing your mind in the area of healing. However, you could have done that without the affliction. Remember sickness and disease affecting your body can be a great motivator! Sickness and disease are a distraction to the believer. It keeps them operating in the plan of God for their life. Sickness is a manifestation of death and bondage. You cannot fully complete the will of God when bound.

Is my suffering glorifying God?

God can better use you if you are not suffering. Suffering consumes you and gets your focus on the suffering and not on your God. People often become so attached to their suffering that they actually develop a soul tie with it. It becomes their identity. Our identity should only come from God. For some the suffering gives them a reason to solicit pity and resources. Some use their suffering as an avenue for manipulation. This is one way that the enemy uses to take advantage of us.

God does not need you to suffer to prove your love for Him. The last person who suffered for our sin, sickness, and disease was Jesus. He suffered for us, so we did not have to. Our suffering ended in Him. When we say, we are suffering for him, we are denying the work of Christ on the cross (1 Peter 2:24 AMP).

Will my healing only come if it is God's will? If God thinks it's time for me to go, I will go.

Faith begins where the will of God is known. If you do not believe that it is the will of God to heal you, you will not see the manifestation of healing in your life. Healing is in the salvation package as we previously discussed. God gives you a free will. He will allow what you allow. He has given you authority (Luke 10:19). If you choose to submit your authority to Satan by believing the lie, God will allow you to do so. God wants you to fulfill the length of your days and the purposes He has called you to. He has provided the truth in the Word of God. You must avail yourself to it and accept its instructions and promises. God wants you to live and not die (Psalm 118:17). God gets no glory by you dying before your time or dying with sickness and disease. This belief is based in fear and ignorance.

Does it mean I don't believe God or am not in faith if I go to the doctor or take medicine/medical treatment?

God created doctors and medicine. He can work through these avenues toward healing. By having a health care background, I personally believe with the state of medicine today with its numerous errors it can take more faith to believe in doctors and medical science! However, God heals in many ways. The key is to ask God what should you do? At times our soul, (mind, will, and emotions) can be so entangled with the thoughts of the sickness/disease, that we might just have to follow peace or sound, godly counsel. This is one of the many reasons every believer should be submitted to a local church or assembly.

You can use your faith while going to the doctor. Believers do not have to be afraid of the doctor. I am a large proponent of utilizing the medical services available to you. As believers, we must operate in wisdom. It is wisdom to get your annual checkups and physicals. When something does not seem right in your body, pray AND go to see your doctor. Often your doctor can give you a diagnosis, or what you need to focus your faith. He can offer natural wisdom to add to your faith. Maybe you need to make dietary changes or let go of stress? These things are good to know. Living in a state of sickness with no medical intervention can cause worse instances in your body. This can leave you hospitalized, needing surgery, or even lead to death. Too many well-meaning Christians die before their time due to ignorance. Even Jesus traveled with a doctor, Luke.

God wants you well. He wants you to live in divine health. He wants you whole. It is an incomplete gospel to ignore these truths. Living a healthy life, eating right, exercising, and avoiding stress may be hard on your flesh, and it requires discipline, but the rewards cannot be matched.

If sickness is not the will of God, then why did Paul have a thorn in the flesh? He also was blind on the Road to Damascus. He suffered with sickness.

Earlier in this chapter, we discussed the term "cognitive dissonance". As a review, cognitive dissonance is the mental discomfort a person can experience when presented with differing or contradictory beliefs to their own. If you already have a belief that sickness is not God's will, you look at information with that filter. Therefore, you rationalize information that you are presented with to agree with your previous belief. In this case, individuals use Paul's situation as evidence that it is not God's will to heal.

There is a belief that Paul had a disease that God "refused" to heal (2 Cor. 12:7-10). People use this as an excuse for having a long-term illness. However, Paul's thorn in the flesh was not a physical illness. He was contending with a demonic spirit that was sent to oppose him in his purpose of spreading the gospel. The text reads "the **messenger** of Satan to buffet me". The word "messenger" denotes an entity. The reason why Satan sent a "messenger" was Paul's "abundance of revelations". The Bible also speaks of how Satan sends affliction and persecution for the Word's sake (Mark 4:16-17). This thorn was manifested in persecution or pressure which was brought about due to people.

During Paul's radical conversion experience, he did suffer blindness on the Road to Damascus. However, in Acts 9:17-18 Ananias laid hands on Paul and he received his sight. He was also filled with the Holy Spirit. After which he became a powerful witness of Christ. Therefore, after being healed by God, he was stronger and able to fulfill God's purpose for his life. If sickness was God's will, wouldn't He have left him sick? However, we can see here that this was not the case, and God needed Paul healed, whole, and well.

What about Job?

Satan caused the destruction in Job's life. Job attributed this to God. Why? Job had no reference point for Satan. He did not even know Satan existed, therefore, he attributed the destruction and sickness to God (Job 2:7). Satan is the accuser; Jesus intercedes for us (Rom 8:31-39). I personally believe in Job's case that there was an open door in his life which allowed Satan to get an advantage over him. Job's story teaches us many things about patience, endurance, and forgiveness. It chronicles the emotions that can spring up when presented with consistent tragedy. However, in the end, God restored Job to greater than what he previously had once he got his heart right (Job 42:10-12).

Examining Your Answers

Have you lived your life based on erroneous answers to these questions? If your answer to this question is yes; just commit today to start fresh. Starting fresh first means forgiving yourself and those that led you into the error. Next, study your Word (2 Timothy 2:15). Get a revelation for yourself concerning these truths. Uprooting this type of thinking will take work. You may be dismantling years of strongholds that have been built in your mind and heart. We discussed strongholds in Chapters 3 and 4. Go back to those chapters and use the tools there in your journey of walking in the truth of God's Word.

You must examine what exactly is your truth. Is your truth based in the Word of God or is it based in your experience or opinion? These can be hard questions to ask ourselves. However, the answers to these questions could mean life or death to us or those we love. Our truth must be based in the Word of God. Discover truth for yourself and expect healing to manifest in your life.

Activation Prayer

Father, I pray you reveal and expose my erroneous beliefs about healing. Reveal to me where I have missed it when seeking healing for myself and for others. Help me to search your Word for the truth. I pray that you give me the spirit of wisdom and revelation in the knowledge of you and that the eyes of my understanding will be enlightened. I thank you that you are helping me to dismantle strongholds which have hindered me in my walk with Christ especially concerning healing. I thank you Lord that you are a faithful God that hears and answers my prayers. In Jesus's name. Amen

Next Steps

1. Go to http://bit.ly/gshbookbonus (password: healing) and download the Truth vs Error Guide based on the information in this chapter. Fill out the worksheet and chart your beliefs.

2. Continue using your guide and take each erroneous belief and study the Word for yourself. Watch the video "How to Study the Bible" if you have never studied the Word to gain understanding.

3. Pray the Pauline prayers for yourself. You can find a copy and instructional video at http://bit.ly/gshbookbonus (password: healing). These are the prayers that Paul prayed for his churches throughout the New Testament. Have an expectation to receive greater revelation of the Word as a result.

Prescription for Divine Health: Practice Healthy Habits

Commit to practicing healthy habits. One of the best things you can do for your health is practicing overall healthy habits. These include getting adequate sleep (6-8 hours), exercise most days of the week, drinking water, reducing stress, and healthy eating. I believe a person's health is a very individual. Each of our bodies has unique characteristics. It is best for you to consult with your doctor as to the best eating and exercise regimen which works best for your body. Pick one habit to begin and start there.

CHAPTER 6

So, What Now? Next Steps

You have reached the end of this book. You have journeyed through and received inspiration and revelation of God's wonderful plan of divine healing and health for His children. I pray in just reading this book you have received healing and deliverance. If this is the case, please send us your testimony, so we can rejoice with you! You can contact us via the web/email addresses found at the end of this book.

The Process of Healing

For some, your healing might be more of a process. A process of God healing you layer by layer. It will take your partnership with the spirit of God, accountability to a mature believer, further study in God's Word, and discipleship. For some, professional Biblically based counseling is needed. You must be real with yourself and where you are in your journey of healing. Take the necessary steps to walk in complete healing. Some of us have been so deeply wounded emotionally that a team of believers is necessary to walk us through our healing. There is no shame in love. It is the love of God to submit to His process of healing. You must do your work. Do your part and God will add His super to your natural steps. Pride will keep you from walking in the fullness of what God has for you every time!

This book is designed to give you a good foundation to grow. Growth typically happens in community. The foundation of a thriving community is a life-giving church. A life-giving church is one where the spirit of God is present, where the word of God is taught and preached. It is a church where you can come as you are and receive healing through the love of God exemplified through its membership. A life-giving church has systematic processes in place to build community like small groups. Submit to the process of your healing.

The Word of God is Your Anchor

An essential tool in developing in your healing journey is the Word of God. The Word of God will be an anchor to your soul (mind, will and emotions). The Word of God is what you will stand on when the enemy attacks you with symptoms of sickness and disease. At times, we can receive from God by a gift of the spirit. However, the Word of God and the spirit are needed to live a successful Christian life. As believers, we have to be proficient in the Word of God to stand against the attacks of the enemy.

> *In conclusion, be strong in the Lord [be empowered through your union with Him]; draw your strength from Him [that strength which His boundless might provides]. Put on God's whole armor [the armor of a heavy-armed soldier which God supplies], that you may be able successfully to stand up against [all] the strategies and the deceits of the devil. For we are not wrestling with flesh and blood [contending only with physical opponents], but against the despotisms, against the powers, against [the master spirits who are] the world rulers of this present darkness, against the spirit forces of wickedness in the heavenly (supernatural) sphere. Therefore, put on God's complete armor, that you may be able to resist and stand your ground on the evil day [of danger], and, having done all [the crisis demands], to stand [firmly in your place].*

Stand therefore [hold your ground], having tightened the belt of truth around your loins and having put on the breastplate of integrity and of moral rectitude and right standing with God, And having shod your feet in preparation [to face the enemy with the firm-footed stability, the promptness, and the readiness produced by the good news] of the Gospel of peace. Lift up over all the [covering] shield of saving faith, upon which you can quench all the flaming missiles of the wicked [one]. And take the helmet of salvation and the sword that the Spirit wields, which is the Word of God. Pray at all times (on every occasion, in every season) in the Spirit, with all [manner of] prayer and entreaty. To that end keep alert and watch with strong purpose and perseverance, interceding in behalf of all the saints (God's consecrated people).

-- Ephesians 6:10-18 AMPC

The armor of God is a necessary tool in your Christian life and your healing journey. When dealing with long-time illness, we have to be consistent in our ability to contend with the enemy. The enemy attempts to use sickness and disease to get us to identify with it, and our symptoms instead of Christ and the finished work on the Cross. This finished work paid the price for our healing. However, we must remain steadfast in our faith and listening to the voice of God for our directions.

Jesus is the Key to Healing, Freedom and Restoration

The Spirit of God will lead, guide, and direct you on your journey of healing and total restoration. In this book, we did not explicitly tackle the subject of restoration. However, restoration is a part of healing. Expect to receive back and in overflow what the enemy has stolen from you due to the sickness and disease you have been facing or have overcome. God will give you more than you had before. Your final state will be greater than your original condition. A Biblical example of this is Job. The enemy afflicted Job with many things. He lost all that he had and even his family. However, the Bible says that the Lord restored Job and gave him more than he had in the beginning (Job 42:10-12).

Some of you reading this book are or have been in a situation similar to Job where the enemy has afflicted you with sickness and disease to the point that it has robbed you of your purpose, finances, friends, and family. However, God is a God of restoration, and He can and will restore all that was lost. You just have to believe and expect him to do it. You must submit to the direction of God and wise counsel. You must be real with yourself, repent for anything you have done or are doing to hinder the hand of God, and commit to completely surrender to Jesus.

Ultimately, Jesus is the key to your healing, deliverance, and restoration. The tools and information found in this book are good. However, if you throw it all out and focus on developing a real and intimate relationship with Jesus, healing, health, and restoration will be the byproducts. The more time you spend in the presence of God and in the Word of God will cause your healing to come quickly. In doing this, you must have the right motivation. God is looking at your heart. We must not seek God simply for what He can do for us but seek God because we love Him. Your time with God should not be for the sole purpose of attaining healing from Him.

When you get to know God intimately, you will find that you enjoy His presence and being with Him. You will long to be with Him (Psalm 63). There might be some reading this that do not have a personal relationship with Jesus Christ or have let their relationship grow silent. If this is you, your relationship can easily be gained or restored. Maybe you feel as though you have not lived a very good life and God would never accept you as a child. That is a lie from the devil. God accepts all who come to Him with a sincere and repentant heart.

Get in a quiet place and talk to God yourself. Tell him you repent for your actions which are not in line with His Word. Ask for his forgiveness from your sins. The Bible says that if we confess or tell God our sins that He is faithful to forgive us (1 John 1:9; Romans 10:8-10). The Word also says that we have an advocate with Jesus Christ. He was the sacrifice for our sins (1 John 2:1-2). Jesus went to the Father on our behalf presenting what He did for us on the cross to wash away our past, present, and future sins by his death on the cross (John 3:16). If you have not asked Jesus to come into your heart and save you, do so now. Tell God that you believe that He sent His son, Jesus, to die for your sins. Tell Him you believe that Jesus rose from the dead and is alive right now with God.

Once you ask for forgiveness, accept by faith that you are forgiven, and your sins are under the blood of Jesus. Now it is time to start your new or renewed walk with Jesus Christ. Go to Him and tell Him your most intimate thoughts and feelings. He will listen and guide you by His Holy Spirit. Learn more about God and His son, Jesus, by reading about Him in the Bible. The Bible describes the character of God. Start in the book of John in the New Testament and get a version online or in print which you can understand like the Amplified version or the New Living translation. Congratulations! You are on your way to living your best life!

If you made a decision for Christ or reestablished your relationship with Him, tell us about it. You can contact me via any of my online social media accounts or by email on my website. All my contact information can be found in the back of this book. Also, click on this link, http://bit.ly/gshbookbonus (password: healing) to receive the amazing book bonuses to help you walk out your divine health and healing and live a fabulous life!

Notes

Chapter 1
Is Healing God's Will?

1. G2137 – euodoō – Strong's Greek Lexicon (KJV). "Blue Letter Bible". Retrieved from https://www.blueletterbible.org//lang/lexicon/lexicon.cfm?Strongs=G2137&t=KJV (Accessed July 7, 2017).

2. G5198 – hygiainō – Strong's Greek Lexicon (KJV). "Blue Letter Bible". Retrieved from https://www.blueletterbible.org//lang/lexicon/lexicon.cfm?Strongs=G5198&t=KJV (Accessed July 7, 2017).

3. The term "sonship" is used as a generalized term in this sense regardless of gender.

4. "G4102 – pistis – Strong's Greek Lexicon (KJV). "Blue Letter Bible". Retrieved from https://www.blueletterbible.org//lang/lexicon/lexicon.cfm?Strongs=G4102&t=KJV (Accessed July 7, 2017).

5. G5287 – hypostasis – Strong's Greek Lexicon (KJV). "Blue Letter Bible". Retrieved from https://www.blueletterbible.org//lang/lexicon/lexicon.cfm?Strongs=G5287&t=KJV (Accessed July 7, 2017).

6. G1679 – elpizō – Strong's Greek Lexicon (KJV). "Blue Letter

Bible". Retrieved from https://www.blueletterbible.org//lang/lexicon/lexicon.cfm?Strongs=G1679&t=KJV (Accessed July 7, 2017).

7. G1650 – clegchos – Strong's Greek Lexicon (KJV). "Blue Letter Bible". Retrieved from https://www.blueletterbible.org//lang/lexicon/lexicon.cfm?Strongs=G1650&t=KJV (Accessed July 7, 2017).

8. G101 – adynateō – Strong's Greek Lexicon (KJV). "Blue Letter Bible". Retrieved from https://www.blueletterbible.org//lang/lexicon/lexicon.cfm?Strongs=G101&t=KJV (Accessed July 7, 2017).

9. G3406 – misthapodotēs – Strong's Greek Lexicon (KJV). "Blue Letter Bible". Retrieved from https://www.blueletterbible.org//lang/lexicon/lexicon.cfm?Strongs=G3406&t=KJV (Accessed July 7, 2017).

10. G1567 – ekzēteō – Strong's Greek Lexicon (KJV). "Blue Letter Bible". Retrieved from https://www.blueletterbible.org//lang/lexicon/lexicon.cfm?Strongs=G1567&t=KJV (Accessed July 7, 2017).

11. "Appropriate" http://www.dictionary.com/browse/appropriate (Accessed July 7, 2017).

Chapter 2

I Don't Have Enough Faith to be Healed

1. H1897 – hagah – Strong's Hebrew Lexicon (KJV). "Blue Letter Bible". https://www.blueletterbible.org//lang/lexicon/lexicon.cfm?Strongs=H1897&t=KJV (Accessed June 18, 2016.)

2. "What is a Schema?" By Kendra Cherry http://psychology.about.com/od/sindex/g/def_schema.htm (Accessed January 2, 2016)

3. Bartlett, F.C. (1932). *Remembering: A Study in Experimental and Social Psychology*. Cambridge, England: Cambridge University Press.

4. Piaget, J. (1928). *The Child's Conception of the World*. London: Routledge and Kegan Paul.

5. Ibid

6. G4964 – syschēmatizō – Strong's Greek Lexicon (KJV). "Blue Letter Bible". https://www.blueletterbible.org//lang/lexicon/lexicon.cfm?Strongs=G4964&t=KJV (Accessed September 27, 2016).

7. Greek Lexicon: G3339 (KJV). "Blue Letter Bible." http://www.blueletterbible.org. https://www.blueletterbible.org/lang/lexicon/lexicon.cfm (Accessed January 2, 2016).

Chapter 4

The Nature and Character of God

1. Webster's 1828 Dictionary. www.webstersdictionary1828.com (Retrieved January 11, 2017)

2. Kenyon, E.W. (1999). – *Two Kinds of Righteousness*. Lynnwood, Washington: Kenyon's Gospel Publishing Society, Inc., 12.

3. G4982 – sōzō – Strong's Greek Lexicon (KJV). "Blue Letter Bible". Retrieved from https://www.blueletterbible.org//lang/lexicon/lexicon.cfm?Strongs=G4982&t=KJV (Accessed September 26, 2017)

Chapter 5

Questions About Healing

1. Festinger, L. (1957). *A Theory of Cognitive Dissonance*. California: Stanford University Press. Festinger, L. (1962). "Cognitive dissonance". *Scientific American*. 207 (4): 93–107. doi:10.1038/

scientificamerican1062-93

2. G4982 – sōzō – Strong's Greek Lexicon (KJV). "Blue Letter Bible". Retrieved from https://www.blueletterbible.org//lang/lexicon/lexicon.cfm?Strongs=G4982&t=KJV (Accessed October 25, 2017)

About the Author

Dr. Andrea is committed to partnering with you to live in divine health and healing. Dr. Andrea is an entrepreneur, licensed minister and health educator. She has over 15 years' experience teaching, training, and inspiring others in the areas of health, wellness, and biblical-based divine healing. Andrea holds a doctorate in education, a master's in public health, and bachelor's in psychology/pre-medicine. She is a nationally certified health education specialist, college administrator and professor. She is an avid runner and wife to Royce Hart Jr. Royce and Dr. Andrea reside in Jacksonville, Florida.

Connect with Me!

Facebook: God Still Heals with Dr. Andrea

Facebook Private Group (Free): God Still Heals with Dr. Andrea

Instagram: dr_andreaihart

Twitter/Periscope: dr_andreaihart

LinkedIn: https://www.linkedin.com/in/andreaihart/

Email: contact@drandreihart.com

Blog/Website: www.drandreaihart.com

Made in United States
Orlando, FL
07 March 2025

59258672R00059